HOW TO PASS

DATA INTERPRETATION TESTS

D0771731

HOW TO PASS

DATA INTERPRETATION TESTS

Unbeatable practice for numerical and quantitative reasoning and problem solving tests

MIKE BRYON

KOGAN PAGE

London and Philadelphia

Publisher's note

Every possible effort has been made to ensure that the information contained in this book is accurate at the time of going to press, and the publishers and authors cannot accept responsibility for any errors or omissions, however caused. No responsibility for loss or damage occasioned to any person acting, or refraining from action, as a result of the material in this publication can be accepted by the editor, the publisher or the author.

First published in Great Britain and the United States in 2009 by Kogan Page Limited

120 Pentonville Road
London N1 9JN
United Kingdom
www.koganpage.com

525 South 4th Street, #241
Philadelphia PA 19147
USA

© Mike Bryon, 2009

ISBN 978 0 7494 4970 4

British Library Cataloguing-in-Publication Data

A CIP record for this book is available from the British Library.

Library of Congress Cataloging-in-Publication Data

Bryon, Mike.
  How to pass data interpretation tests : unbeatable practice for numerical and quantitative reasoning and problem solving tests / Mike Bryon.
      p. cm.
    ISBN 978-0-7494-4970-4
1. Psychometrics. 2. Numeracy—Problems, exercises, etc. 3. Employment tests I. Title.
  BF39.B78 2009
  153.9′3--dc22
                                                    2009017478

Typeset by Saxon Graphics Ltd, Derby
Printed and bound in India by Replika Press Pvt Ltd

Contents

Preface

This book provides everything you need for a successful programme of revision or review. It contains 330 practice questions with answers and explanations, advice on how to show your true potential and signposts to sources of further practice material.

Tests of data interpretation are fast becoming the most common type of psychometric test. They feature in the recruitment process for many positions in the professional services, finance, accountancy and graduate traineeships, and jobs including firefighter and many of those in the UK Civil Service. They can feature at any point in the process. In some instances they are taken online, often at the beginning of the recruitment process; in other instances they occur as a part of a battery of psychometric tests midway through the process. They also feature towards the end of some selection processes as a task at an assessment centre. In all instances they comprise a series of data sets drawn from almost any discipline to which a series of numeric questions relate. It is your task to extract the appropriate data, demonstrate good judgement and undertake any necessary calculations in order to select the correct answer from the list of suggested answers.

You will not find another book with so many practice questions on this subject, nor one so completely up to date and relevant to data interpretation tests used today. Uniquely, it offers 20 timed mini tests so that you can practise the all-important start to a data interpretation test and approach a real test with a new confidence.

Data interpretation tests and the winning approach

We face psychometric tests at so many points in our career and their use is on the increase. Psychometric tests of your numerical skills are by far the most widespread type and data interpretation tests are fast becoming the most common sort of numerical test. They are administered at a computer terminal, online or with paper and pen. The test may feature as a standalone assessment or one of a series of sub-tests taken one after the other. Nowadays the majority of recruitment processes will include a data interpretation test.

These tests present you with a series of sets of data made up of, for example, a table, passage, graph or chart. The subject of the majority of these data sets will relate to the workplace and to business. However, expect the unexpected, because the subject can be drawn from every and any discipline. In many instances the data comprise a multiple of data sets and in many instances a passage of information setting the context. In some tests the amount of data presented is extensive and much is irrelevant, so you must filter through the material quickly to find the relevant items. Every set of data is followed by a series of questions, each with a list of suggested answers. You have to sift through this information, combining relevant data from the respective sources, and select one of the suggested answers. In order to identify the correct answer you have to demonstrate good judgement and undertake calculations.

You are expected to answer the questions using only the information contained in the data set. Be careful if you know something about the subject or if you believe the data to be factually incorrect, controversial or out of date. It is not a test of your general knowledge, your knowledge of the last findings in the discipline or your political views. So feel completely as ease about answering a question using the data provided, even if you believe they are false given what you learnt at university or read in a newspaper that morning.

If you face a data interpretation test online or administered at a computer screen then be aware that diagrams on the computer screen can sometimes appear misleading, especially in the case of geometric shapes, tables and graphs, as the screen in some instances can distort the image or the scale or both! The test author is aware of this and will have provided sufficient information to arrive at the answer. So if you are unlucky enough to find a distorted image or find its scale hard to read then rely on the written information and avoid drawing unnecessary assumptions about the appearance of a diagram, table or graph on the screen. For example, if a shape is described as a cube but on the screen the sides do not all seem equal, ignore it and treat the shape as a cube. Equally, if a table or graph says that quantity x is the largest but on the screen it looks like quantity y is the same or in fact bigger, take no notice and treat quantity x as the largest.

If until now you have struggled with maths and you have to pass such a test to realize your career or educational goal then it is time to get down to some serious score-improving practice. Everyone can rise to the challenge and master these questions – some have to practise more than others. A few will have to show a great deal of determination and work very hard.

This book is suitable for all levels from intermediate to advanced. You will find hundreds more practice questions in the following titles from the Kogan Page testing series:

More at the intermediate level:

The Numeracy Test Workbook
Ultimate Psychometric Tests
The Verbal Reasoning Test Workbook
How to Pass Diagrammatic Reasoning Tests

At the advanced level:

How to Pass Advanced Numeracy Tests, Revised Edition
How to Pass Graduate Psychometric Tests, 3rd Edition
The Graduate Psychometric Test Workbook
The Advanced Numeracy Test Workbook, 2nd Edition
How To Pass Advanced Verbal Reasoning Tests

If you face a data interpretation test as a part of a recruitment process then expect lots of other people to have applied also. In these circumstances treat the test as a competition and set out to achieve the best score possible. Doing well in a real test is largely down to practice beforehand and working very hard during the test itself.

Start your programme of preparation by understanding exactly what the test involves. The organization that invited you should have provided you with, or directed you to, a description of it and a description of the sorts of question it comprises. Armed with this information, set out to find hundreds of practice questions on which to undertake a systematic programme of preparation. You need hundreds because to get the most out of the practice you should undertake a minimum of 20 hours' practice. If you are weak at maths then be prepared to undertake a lot more than this. The best sort of practice is on material that is as similar to the real questions as possible. Practice, to be effective, must also be challenging, painful even. To be sure that you are continuing to improve, make sure that the practice remains a challenge. If it stops being a pain there really will be very little gain. Practise right up to the day before the test.

Success in every sort of psychometric test also requires the right mental approach. Perhaps you know that you can do the job, and naturally ask yourself why you have to pass a test. You might wonder what relevance it has to the role for which you have applied. These are understandable and common sentiments. But you really must try to put them aside as they are counterproductive and will serve only to distract you from the task of passing the test. If you turn up on the day harbouring resentments then you are unlikely to demonstrate your true potential. The winning candidate inevitably concentrates not on the threat or inconvenience but on the opportunity the test represents. Pass it and you can go on to realize your personal goals. Let your determination to do well in the test take over your life for a few weeks.

Appreciate that doing well in a test is not simply a matter of intelligence. Attend fully prepared and then you can approach the test as a chance to show how strong a candidate you are, confident in your own ability and ready to succeed. If you have experienced failure in the past, if you have previously tried and failed to master these skills, then it will take courage to make the necessary commitment. Understand that they are testing you! Find the strength of character to rise up to that test and you will have demonstrated the exact qualities they are looking for and qualities of which you can be justly proud. Do not underestimate how long it can take to prepare for a test. Start as soon as you receive notice that you must attend.

How you conduct yourself during the test is obviously equally important. You must seek to achieve the very best possible score. If at the end of the test you do not feel fatigued then you may not have done yourself justice. So go for it.

Some very accomplished candidates do not do very well in these tests. Before they can realize a score equal to their achievements they must unlearn a careful considered approach. An approach where you double-check every question only to be told to stop when you have attempted only a small portion of the total questions is not a winning strategy. A good score requires a balance between getting questions right and answering most if not all of the questions. Some candidates therefore only succeed once they risk getting some questions wrong by working through the questions at a much faster rate.

If you hit a difficult section of questions, do not lose heart. Keep going – every candidate gets some questions wrong. You may well find that the next set of questions is of a type in which you can excel.

It often pays to approximate answers in order to speed up calculations and to eliminate some of the suggested answers as wrong. If you do not know the answer to a question then educated guessing can pay and features in the test strategy of many successful candidates. If you are unsure of an answer to a multiple choice question then look at the suggested answers and try to rule some out as wrong. In this way you will reduce the number of suggested answers from which to choose and hopefully increase your chances of guessing correctly.

If you are finding it difficult to identify sufficient further practice material or if you would like advice on a specific aspect of the recruitment process or test that you face, then by all means e-mail me at help@mikebryon.com and I will be happy to respond to your query.

One hundred and forty warm-up data interpretation questions

This chapter comprises 140 warm-up questions. The idea is that you can ease yourself into the style and format of the questions and build up your familiarity, accuracy and confidence. Some but no means all of these questions are easier than the questions that make up a real data interpretation test. This is why they are called warm-up questions. They will allow many candidates to learn or revise key competencies and become familiar with the challenge. With time this practice will build confidence, comprehension and skills to the point where they are able to tackle questions at the level of the real thing.

Speed is not of the essence when it comes to these warm-up questions. We will practise building speed in the next chapter, so use this material to become completely confident in interpreting data, reasoning with it and making the required calculations.

Use as much scrap or scratch paper as you need, but do not use a calculator.

Data set 1: The Lagoon Hotel

Guests staying at the Lagoon Hotel choose a two- or five-day package and select on either package either accommodation only, half board or full board. On one evening the hotel has a total of 48 guests, 17 of whom have chosen the two-day package. Of the remaining guests (on the five-day package), 16 have opted for accommodation only while 3 have selected half board.

Additional information:

- That night a total of 21 guests had selected accommodation only.
- In total, 20 guests have selected full board.

1. On the evening in question, how many guests had selected the five-day package?
   A 28
   B 29
   C 30
   D 31

   Answer ☐

2. How many guests staying in the hotel that evening on the five-day package had selected full board?
   A 12
   B 19
   C 20
   D 21

   Answer ☐

3. How many guests on the two-day package had selected accommodation only?

    A   5

    B   17

    C   21

    D   There is insufficient information to answer the question.

    Answer

4. Of the guests who had selected full board, how many were on the two-day package?

    A   1

    B   8

    C   11

    D   19

    Answer

5. In total, how many guests that evening had selected half board?

    A   3

    B   5

    C   7

    D   9

    Answer

6. · How many guests on the two-day package selected half board?

    A   8

    B   5

    C   4

    D   2

    Answer

7. Which statement is true?
    A   On the five-day package twice as many people are half
        board compared to full board.
    B   On the two-day package twice as many people are half
        board compared to full board.
    C   On the five-day package half as many people are on half
        board compared to full board.
    D   On the two-day package half as many people are on half
        board compared to full board.

                                            Answer

8. How many people on the two-day package are NOT on full
    board?
    A   8
    B   9
    C   10
    D   11

                                            Answer

9. Which is the most popular option?
    A   Accommodation only on the five-day package
    B   Full board on the five-day package
    C   Full board on the two-day package
    D   Half board on the two-day package

                                            Answer

10. What fraction of the total number of guests opted for full
    board on the five-day package?
    A   1/2
    B   1/5
    C   1/3
    D   1/4

                                            Answer

Data set 2: Means of travel to work

The findings of a survey into how people travel to work (presented as both a bar and a pie chart) are shown below.

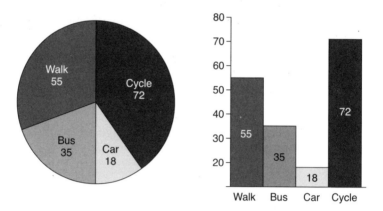

Note:

1 in 8 of the people who cycled to work were found to be over 65 years of age.

1 in 3 of the cyclists stated that they travelled to work by bus on rainy days.

11. How many more respondents indicated that they walked to work rather than travelled by bus?

   A   55
   B   35
   C   20
   D   18

   Answer ☐

12. How many more people indicated that they cycled to work compared with those who travelled by either bus or car?
    A 72
    B 35
    C 18
    D 19

    Answer ☐

13. What is the total number of responses represented in the survey?
    A 180
    B 170
    C 160
    D 150

    Answer ☐

14. The sum of which categories, if any, represents half the number of responses represented in the survey?
    A Cycle and car
    B Bus and car
    C Walk and bus
    D Walk and cycle

    Answer ☐

15. How many degrees of arc in the pie chart represent each response in the survey results?
    A 8°
    B 6°
    C 4°
    D 2°

    Answer ☐

16. Which of the following best represents the ratio of responses between car and cycle?
    A   1 : 6
    B   1 : 5
    C   1 : 4
    D   1 : 3

    Answer

17. What fraction most closely represents the segment of the pie labelled bus?
    A   1/2
    B   1/4
    C   1/5
    D   1/6

    Answer

18. Which of the following statements is true?
    A   Slightly fewer than twice as many people indicated that they travelled to work by bus than by car.
    B   Slightly more than twice as many people indicated that they travelled to work by bus than by car.
    C   Slightly more people indicated that they travelled to work by bus than by car.
    D   Slightly fewer people indicated that they travelled to work by car than by bus.

    Answer

19. How many respondents indicated that they cycled to work and were over 65 years old?
    A   12
    B   9
    C   8
    D   Cannot tell

    Answer

20. How many people cycled on a rainy day?
   A 24
   B 48
   C 72
   D Cannot tell

   Answer ☐

Data set 3: Sea breezes, balls, balloons and submarines

A balloon will return to its original shape after it has been stretched and a ball will return to its original shape after it has been compressed. A dough- or paste-like substance, for example bread dough or toothpaste, when compressed and stretched will not return to its original shape. Balloons and balls are said to be elastic while a dough or paste is said to be plastic.

A submarine alters its weight by adjusting the amount of air or water in its ballast tanks. This way it can remain at a given depth, rise or sink in the water. The principle behind the submarine's manoeuvres can be described as upward force = weight of submarine.

A sea breeze involves the transfer of heat by convection. At the coast during the day the land warms faster than the sea and this causes air over the land to warm and rise; cooler air from over the sea then moves in to replace the air over the land that has risen. At night the land cools faster than the sea and so the process is reversed.

   $<$ means less than, eg $3 < 4$
   $>$ means greater than, eg $5 > 4$
   $\geq$ means greater than or equal to
   $\leq$ means less than or equal to

21. The elasticity of a balloon > the elasticity of a paste.
    A   True
    B   False
    C   Cannot tell

    Answer

22. The speed at which land warms is < the speed at which water warms.
    A   True
    B   False
    C   Cannot tell

    Answer

23. When a submarine sinks, the upward force > the submarine's weight.
    A   True
    B   False
    C   Cannot tell

    Answer

24. The sea cools at a rate > than the land.
    A   True
    B   False
    C   Cannot tell

    Answer

25. When a submarine rises, the upward force > than the submarine's weight.
    A   True
    B   False
    C   Cannot tell

    Answer

26. When a submarine rises, the amount of water is $<$ air in its ballast tanks.
    A   True
    B   False
    C   Cannot tell

    Answer ☐

27. The plasticity of a dough $<$ the plasticity of a ball.
    A   True
    B   False
    C   Cannot tell

    Answer ☐

28. A dough has $\leq$ elasticity compared to a paste.
    A   Probably true
    B   Probably false
    C   Cannot tell

    Answer ☐

29. At night the air temperature over the sea is $\geq$ to the temperature of the air over the land.
    A   Probably true
    B   Probably false
    C   Cannot tell

    Answer ☐

30. When a submarine remains at a given depth the weight of the submarine equals the upward force.
    A   True
    B   False
    C   Cannot tell

    Answer ☐

Data set 4: Distribution of women across professional and managerial grades

The distribution of women across professional and managerial grades in 'Not Yet There' Corporation is shown below.

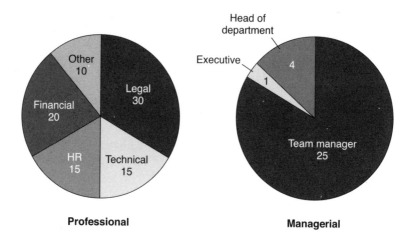

Professional   **Managerial**

HR = Human Resources

Note:

There are five times as many men in professional grades as women. The corporation employs a total of 1,300 staff in both professional and managerial grades.

8% of the total workforce at the corporation is employed in professional and managerial grades.

31. How many women hold professional grades in 'Not Yet There' Corporation?

    A   120
    B   110
    C   100
    D   90

Answer

32. In total, how many staff (both men and women) are employed in professional grades in the corporation?

    A   540
    B   450
    C   360
    D   270

    Answer

33. What fraction of women in managerial grades is in head of department or executive grades?

    A   1/4
    B   1/5
    C   1/6
    D   1/7

    Answer

34. How many of the total staff in professional and managerial grades are men?

    A   1,210
    B   1,180
    C   1,160
    D   1, 140

    Answer

35. What percentage of women in managerial grades are team managers?

    A   ≥ 80%
    B   ≤ 80%
    C   < 80%
    D   > 80%

    Answer

36. How many more women are there in the grade of team manager than head of department and executive combined?

    A   15

    B   20

    C   25

    D   30

    Answer

37. How many men are in managerial grades?

    A   640

    B   680

    C   730

    D   Cannot tell

    Answer

38. How many people in total does the corporation employ?

    A   16,250

    B   14,950

    C   13,650

    D   Cannot tell

    Answer

39. How many men are in the grade of team manager?

    A   700

    B   698

    C   696

    D   Cannot tell

    Answer

40. What percentage of women in professional grades are in Legal and Human Resources combined?

    A   50%

    B   45%

    C   33%

    D   30%

    Answer

Data set 5: Distances from New Zealand by sea

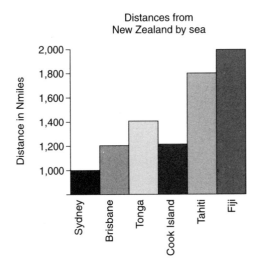

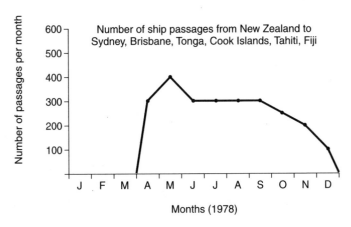

Notes:

An Nmile is a nautical mile and is 10% greater than a mile (used to measure distance on land).

Tropical storms January–March.

Ships only make these passages before or after the tropical storm season.

The month of May offers the best weather conditions.

The southern ocean current runs at 2 knots/hour west to east all year.

Ships on passage to Sydney and Brisbane must push against the southern ocean current.

Ships on passage to Tonga, Cook Islands and Tahiti are carried along by the southern ocean current.

Ships on passage to Fiji cross the current and so experience no counter or favourable effect.

41. The distance by sea from New Zealand to Brisbane and back is:
    A   2,400 Nmiles
    B   > 2,400 Nmiles
    C   < 2,400 Nmiles
    D   Cannot tell

    Answer

42. How many ship passages from New Zealand to Sydney, Brisbane, Tonga, Cook Island, Tahiti and Fiji took place in 1978?
    A   2,550
    B   2,250
    C   2,450
    D   2,400
    E   Cannot tell

    Answer

43. In land miles, what is the distance from New Zealand to Tonga?
    A   1,400 miles
    B   1,440 miles
    C   1,500 miles
    D   1,540 miles
    E   Cannot tell

    Answer

44. If in the month of December half of all the passages that month were to Sydney and the remainder were to Fiji, how many Nmiles would be covered in total?
    A   100,000 Nmiles
    B   150,000 Nmiles
    C   200,000 Nmiles
    D   250,000 Nmiles
    E   Cannot tell

    Answer

45. How far is it from Sydney to Fiji?
    A   3,000 Nmiles
    B   2.000 Nmiles
    C   800 Nmiles
    D   Cannot tell

    Answer

46. Over a 30-day period during the 1978 storm season, 5 days were classed as experiencing storm conditions. What is the ratio of stormy and non-stormy days during this period?
    A   1 : 3
    B   1 : 4
    C   1 : 5
    D   1 : 6

    Answer

47. What proportion of the total passages for the year 1978 was made in the months June, July, August and September?
    A   < Half
    B   > Half
    C   Exactly half
    D   Cannot tell

    Answer

48. Taking account of the distances and the currents, if a ship were to sail to New Zealand to Brisbane return and then New Zealand to Cook Island return at a constant speed, which passage would you expect to be completed the quicker?
A   New Zealand–Brisbane return
B   Both passages would take the same amount of time
C   New Zealand–Cook Island return
D   Cannot tell

Answer ☐

49. If 12% of all passages made in 1978 were to Cook Island, how many sailings were there to this destination that year?
A   306
B   302
C   298
D   294

Answer ☐

50. A ship on passage from New Zealand to Sydney averages 10 Nmiles/hour through the water and 8 Nmiles/hour over the ground. How many hours would the journey take?
A   125 hours
B   120 hours
C   110 hours
D   100 hours

Answer ☐

Data set 6: Facts of light

The visible light spectrum

R	Red	G	Green	V	Violet
O	Orange	B	Blue		
Y	Yellow	I	Indigo		

Light travels through space at a speed of 299,972 km/s but through water 25% slower and through glass a 1/3 slower still. A microscope made from a single lens can magnify between 70 and 375 times while one made from two lenses can magnify up to 1,875 times. A typical pair of binoculars magnifies an object 30 times. When light is refracted by, for example, a prism or a droplet of water, the colours that make up visible light are displayed (this is called the visible light spectrum).

The electromagnetic spectrum

Gamma and x rays	Ultra violet radiation	Visible light V,I,B,G,Y,O,R	Infrared light	Microwaves
Decreasing wave length →				

51. Which colour in the visible light spectrum has the third-longest wavelength?
    A   Red or orange
    B   Yellow or green
    C   Blue or indigo
    D   Cannot tell

    Answer

52. Which is the best estimate of how far light would travel in space in 30 seconds?
    A   900,000 km
    B   3 million km
    C   9 million km
    D   90 million km

    Answer

53. If, using a typical pair of binoculars, a 138m-long object appeared to be 4.2 cm long, how long would it appear to be to the observer without the binoculars?

    A   4.6 cm
    B   1.4 cm
    C   4.6 mm
    D   1.4 mm

    Answer [   ]

54. Which is the best estimate of how far light could travel through water in 20 seconds (assuming you could find enough water)?

    A   6,750,000 km
    B   4,500,000 km
    C   675,000 km
    D   450,000 km

    Answer [   ]

55. How many times more powerful is a microscope made from two lenses than the most powerful single lens microscope?

    A   ×5
    B   ×4.5
    C   ×4
    D   ×3.5

    Answer [   ]

56. How large would an object that was 0.04 mm in size appear to be through a single lens microscope set at the lowest magnification in the range described?

    A   22 mm
    B   24 mm
    C   26 mm
    D   28 mm

    Answer [   ]

57. Select the closest estimate of how long it would take for an object to journey 12 million km in space if it was travelling at a fifth of the speed of light.

   A   40 seconds
   B   1 minute 50 seconds
   C   3 minutes
   D   3 minutes and 20 seconds

   Answer ☐

58. How many times would an object sized 0.0675 mm need to be magnified in order to appear to be 10.125 mm?

   A   ×140
   B   ×150
   C   ×160
   D   ×170

   Answer ☐

59. What is best approximation of the speed of light travelling through glass?

   A   100,000 km/s
   B   75,000 km/s
   C   25,000 km/s
   D   15,000 km/s

   Answer ☐

60. At what speed does light travel through a prism?

   A   299,972 km/s
   B   224,979 km/s
   C   74,993 km/s
   D   Cannot tell

   Answer ☐

Data set 7: Booking a flight

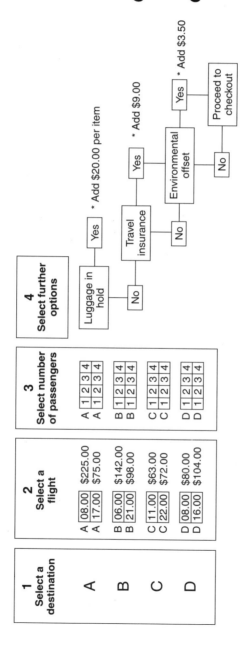

* These additional costs apply to each passenger per flight

61. How much is added to a flight if all options are selected (include only one item of luggage)?
    A $32.50
    B $32.00
    C $31.50
    D $31.00

    Answer ☐

62. How much would be the cost of a flight at 08.00 to destination A for 3 passengers who select none of the further options?
    A $670
    B $675
    C $680
    D $685

    Answer ☐

63. How much more is the morning flight compared with the afternoon flight to destination A, expressed as a multiple?
    A ×3
    B ×4
    C ×5
    D ×6

    Answer ☐

64. How much would be the cost to destination D on the 16.00 flight for a couple who opt for two items of luggage in the hold?
    A $248
    B $260
    C $280
    D $300

    Answer ☐

65. What is the total cost for a party of 54 passengers booked for the morning flight to destination C if one item of hold luggage was booked for each of them?
    A $4,479
    B $4,480
    C $4,481
    D $4,482

    Answer

66. How much more is a morning flight compared with an afternoon flight for a family of four to destination B with travel insurance and three items of hold luggage?
    A $96.00
    B $228.00
    C $44.00
    D $176.00

    Answer

67. A party of three book to fly on the afternoon flight to destination C and opt for two items of hold luggage and the environment offset. How much is the cost of their trip?
    A $266.50
    B $256
    C $226.50
    D $216

    Answer

68. What is the percentage difference between the afternoon and morning flights to destination D?
    A   25%
    B   30%
    C   35%
    D   40%

    Answer

69. A frequent flyer is offered a 20% discount on a single flight which he opts to use on the afternoon flight to destination A. He opts for a single item of luggage in the hold and the environmental offset. The discount applies to the flight only. How much does he pay?

    A $98.50
    B $88.50
    C $83.50
    D $80.50

    Answer [   ]

70. Calculate the range between the maximum and minimum cost of a single journey (with one item of hold luggage)?

    A $174.50
    B $162.00
    C $144.00
    D $134.50

    Answer [   ]

Data set 8: Predicted change in employment by industrial classification

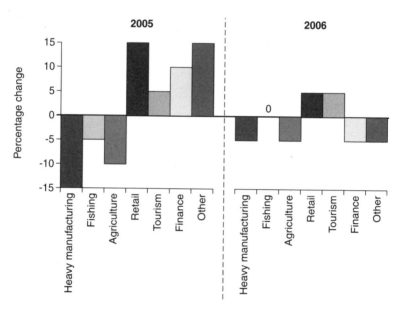

71. In 2005, which industrial classification(s) is/are predicted to increase by the greatest percentage?
    A   Heavy manufacturing and other
    B   Retail
    C   Heavy manufacturing, retail and other
    D   Retail and other

    Answer [ ]

72. By what percentage is fishing predicted to decrease over the two years?
    A   −5%
    B   5%
    C   0%
    D   10%

    Answer [ ]

73. In 2006, which classification is predicted to increase by the least?
    A   Fishing
    B   Finance
    C   Heavy manufacturing
    D   Agriculture

    Answer [ ]

74. In 2006, is a cumulative increase or decrease predicted?
    A   Increase ≥ 10%
    B   Decrease ≤ 10%
    C   Increase ≤ 10%
    D   Decrease ≥ 10%

    Answer [ ]

75. Cumulatively (across the two years), which classification is projected to see the greatest range in % point change?
    A   Heavy manufacturing
    B   Tourism
    C   Other
    D   Finance

    Answer [ ]

76. If 2 million people work in retail, by how many is this predicted to change in 2005?
    A   Decrease by 700,000
    B   Increase by 300,000
    C   Decrease by 300,000
    D   Increase by 700,000

    Answer [ ]

77. In 2005, identify the sector in which the workforce could fall by 37,500 to 712,500.
    A   Fishing
    B   Agriculture
    C   Heavy manufacturing
    D   Cannot tell

    Answer

78. If, at the start of 2005, 2,500,000 work in retail, by how many is this predicted to increase to by the end of 2006?
    A   3 million
    B   2,900,000
    C   Half a million
    D   Cannot tell

    Answer

79. If in total 35 million are employed across the classifications, by how many is this total predicted to change in 2006?
    A   1,750,000 increase
    B   1,750,000 decrease
    C   175,000 decrease
    D   Cannot tell

    Answer

80. In relative terms, which sector is predicted to show the greatest improvement over the two years?
    A   Fishing
    B   Retail
    C   Heavy manufacturing
    D   Cannot tell

    Answer

Data set 9: Mary's Gums

Mary's Gums is a company that sells confectionery in the UK and Irish Republic. The managerial team's revenue targets are presented in the tables. Analyse them to answer the questions that follow.

Revenue 2006 ($000,000)

Fruit salad	1.2
Sour cola	0.7
Cool mints	2.4
Hard gums	1.3
Soft fruit	1.8

$ revenue growth targets for 2007

Fruit salad	24,000
Sour cola	5,250
Cool mints	72,000
Hard gums	6,500
Soft fruit	27,000

% annual revenue growth target for 2008

Fruit salad	3
Sour cola	1
Cool mints	4
Hard gums	2.5
Soft fruit	2

81. What will be the revenue generated from Cool mints in 2007 if the target is realized?

   A $2,472,000
   B $3,120,000
   C $2,407,200
   D $72,002.4

   Answer [　]

82. What is the total revenue for the year 2006?

   A $7,300,000
   B $7,400,000
   C $7,500,000
   D $7,600,000

   Answer [　]

83. What will be the total revenue for the year 2007 if targets are realized?

   A $146,810
   B $7,400,000
   C $7,534,750
   D $7,740,000

   Answer [　]

84. What is the % target increase in revenue in 2008 for the Fruit salad line?

   A   1%
   B   2%
   C   3%
   D   4%

   Answer [　]

85. Which product line has the lowest % revenue growth target for 2007?
    A   Fruit salad
    B   Sour cola
    C   Cool mints
    D   Hard gums
    E   Soft fruit

    Answer

86. Which is the best estimate of the revenue that Sour cola will generate in 2008 if the targets for that year and 2007 are realized?
    A $710,000
    B $711,000
    C $712,000
    D $713,000

    Answer

87. What is the mean target percentage increase for growth in 2008?
    A   2.5%
    B   2.4%
    C   2.3%
    D   2.2%

    Answer

88. If the target during 2007 is realized, how much will the product Hard gums generate in 2006 and 2007 combined?
    A $1,306,500
    B $2,600,500
    C $2,606,500
    D $2,806,500

    Answer

89. In which range does the revenue from Soft fruit in 2008 fall if the targets for that year and 2007 are realized?
    A 1,800,000–1,850,000
    B 1,850,000–1,900,000
    C 1,900,000–1,950,000
    D 1,950,000–2,000,000

    Answer

90. Which of the following statements is NOT valid?
    A Over the 3 years shown, Cool mints is targeted to generate the most revenue.
    B The figures for Hard gums in 2007 and 2008 combined give a target revenue increase of 3%.
    C Over the 3 years shown, Sour cola is targeted to generate the least revenue.
    D The figures for Fruit salad in 2007 and 2008 combined give a target revenue increase of 3%.

    Answer

Data set 10: Railway enquiries

A frequency diagram showing the results of a survey of the duration of telephone conversations at the National Railway Enquires Call Centre over a period of 3 days is given below.

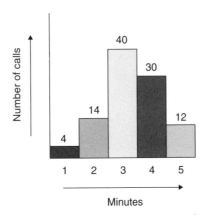

91. How many telephone conversations were included in the survey?

    A   98
    B   99
    C   100
    D   101

    Answer

92. How many telephone conversations lasted 2 minutes or more?

    A   96
    B   70
    C   42
    D   12

    Answer

93. How many telephone conversations lasted more than 1 minute but less than 4?
    A   58
    B   54
    C   44
    D   40

    Answer [ ]

94. Which decimal expresses the probability of a conversation falling into the one-minute range?
    A   0.14
    B   0.4
    C   0.014
    D   1.4

    Answer [ ]

95. Which statement best describes the data in column 2 of the frequency diagram?
    A   14 conversations lasted 2 minutes
    B   14 conversations lasted up to 2 minutes
    C   18 conversations lasted less than 3 minutes
    D   14 conversations lasted more than 1 minute but less than 3 minutes

    Answer [ ]

96. Which fraction expresses the probability of a conversation lasting 3 minutes or more but less than 4?
    A   1/2
    B   2/5
    C   1/3
    D   1/4

    Answer [ ]

97. Which is the best estimate of the length of time spent taking calls in the 3-minute range?
    A   120 minutes
    B   140 minutes
    C   160 minutes
    D   180 minutes

    Answer

98. Which of the following suggestions would NOT improve the accuracy of the survey?
    A   Increase the number of calls surveyed
    B   Conduct the survey over a longer period than 3 days
    C   Inform staff at the centre of the objectives of the survey
    D   Randomly select the calls included in the survey

    Answer

99. Which procedure would provide the mean length of the calls?
    A   Total duration of all calls divided by 100
    B   Total number of calls multiplied by 5
    C $4 \times 1 + 14 \times 2 + 40 \times 3 + 30 \times 4 + 12 \times 5$ divided by the number of calls
    D   Sum of length of all calls multiplied by 100
    E $4 \times 1 + 14 \times 2 + 40 \times 3 + 30 \times 4 + 12 \times 5$ multiplied by the number of calls

    Answer

100. Which of the following estimates of the total time of all conversation is best?
    A   500 minutes
    B   332 minutes
    C   280 minutes
    D   250 minutes

    Answer

Data set 11: Households and their use of instruments of mass media

A graph showing percentage trends in the number of households and their use of particular forms of media over the period 1940–2000 is given below.

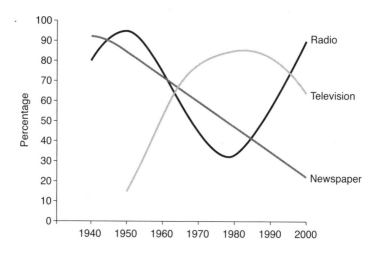

101. In which decade did more than 50% of households first use television?
    A 1960s
    B 1970s
    C 1980s
    D 1990s

    Answer ☐

102. In the 1970s, how many more households used TV rather than radio?
    A Twice as many
    B Two to three times as many
    C Three times as many
    D Cannot say

    Answer ☐

103. During the 1960s there were 30 million households and 70% used radio. How many households is this?
    A   18 million
    B   19 million
    C   20 million
    D   21 million

    Answer ☐

104. In which decade was there a period when all three media were used in approximately equal proportions?
    A   1940s
    B   1950s
    C   1960s
    D   1970s

    Answer ☐

105. Which period could best be described as the golden age of television?
    A   1940s–1980s
    B   1960s–1980s
    C   1950s–1980s
    D   1960s–1990s

    Answer ☐

106. What is the percentage range of households that use newspapers?
    A   20%
    B   50%
    C   70%
    D   90%

    Answer ☐

107. In which two decades was radio used in more households than both television and newspapers?
   A   1950s and 1990s
   B   1940s and 1990s
   C   1940s and 1950s
   D   Cannot tell

   Answer ____

108. In 2000, the graph shows that 90% of households used radio, 60% television and 20% newspapers. If 9 million households used newspapers, how many used radio?
   A   41 million
   B   40.5 million
   C   40 million
   D   39.5 million

   Answer ____

109. In the 30-year period 1970–2000, which medium had the least variation in usage?
   A   Television
   B   Radio
   C   Newspapers
   D   Cannot tell

   Answer ____

110. In their 'heyday' (the 1940s) newspapers were used by 19.8 million (90%) of households. This percentage had halved by the 1980s. How many households was this?
   A   9.9 million
   B   9.8million
   C   9.7 million
   D   Cannot tell

   Answer ____

Data set 12: Marco glass

In recent years sales of Marco glass have not reflected the increase in the number of visitors to Venice, Italy, where the glass is made and sold.

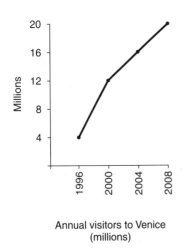

Annual visitors to Venice
(millions)

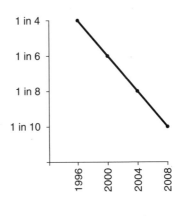

Ratio of visitors who
buy/do not buy Marco glass

Value of annual sales of Marco glass

2000	2002	2004	2006
$50 million	$51 million	$54 million	$55 million

111. What was the total value of sales over the 6-year period?
    A   210 million
    B   315 million
    C   420 million
    D   Cannot tell

Answer

112. By how many did the number of visitors to Venice increase between 2000 and 2004?
    A   2 million
    B   4 million
    C   6 million
    D   8 million

    Answer

113. In the years shown, the number of visitors who buy Marco glass has:
    A   Remained consistent
    B   Been consistent in all years but one
    C   Been inconsistent
    D   Consistently fallen

    Answer

114. How many fewer people bought Marco glass in 1996 compared to 2008?
    A   ×2.5
    B   ×2
    C   ×1.5
    D   ×1

    Answer

115. Which of the following is the correct percentage equivalent to the ratio of visitors to Venice in 2004 who buy/do not buy Marco glass?
    A   17.5%
    B   15%
    C   12.5%
    D   Cannot tell

    Answer

116. How much did the average visitor spend on Marco glass in the year 2000?
    A   Between $4 and $5
    B   Between $8 and $10
    C   Between $17 and $20
    D   Between $24 and $26

    Answer

117. 12% of visitors to Venice in 2000 were from the Far East, which equates to:
    A   940,000
    B   950,000
    C   1,440,000
    D   Cannot tell

    Answer

118. Which of the following statements is it not possible to identify as either true or false?
    A   In 1999 fewer than 1 in 5 visitors bought Marco glass.
    B   In 2001 the value of sales in Marco glass was between $50 and $51 million.
    C   Marco glass is sold worldwide.
    D   Between 1996 and 2008 visitors to Venice grow threefold.

    Answer

119. How much more was the average spend per visitor who bought Marco glass in 2004 than 2000?
    A $2
    B $3
    C $4
    D $5

    Answer

120. If 3 times as many women as men visit Venice, how many women visited in 2008?

    A   4 million
    B   12 million
    C   15 million
    D   Cannot tell

    Answer

Data set 13: Data files

The size of 300 data files

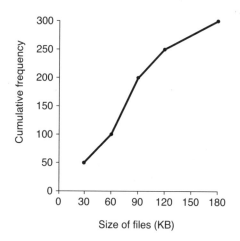

121. How many files are smaller than 30 KB?

    A   150
    B   100
    C   50
    D   30

    Answer

122. How many files are 90 KB or larger?
   A   300
   B   200
   C   100
   D   90

   Answer ☐

123. Which is the best estimate of the median size?
   A   Below 75 KB
   B   Below 90 KB
   C   Below 100 KB
   D   Below 150 KB

   Answer ☐

124. 250 of the files are:
   A   120 KB
   B   Between 100 and 120 KB
   C   Between 90 and 120 KB
   D   Smaller than 120 KB

   Answer ☐

125. How many files are 60 KB or more but less than 90 KB in size?
   A   200
   B   100
   C   30
   D   Cannot tell

   Answer ☐

126. Which is the best estimate of the size of the data files located at the upper quartile line?
   A   225 KB
   B   105 KB
   C   75 KB
   D   112.5 KB

   Answer ☐

127. How many times bigger is a 180 KB file compared with a 30 KB file?
    A ×3
    B ×4
    C ×5
    D ×6

    Answer

128. What is the best estimate for the value of the lower quartile?
    A 75 KB
    B 50 KB
    C 45 KB
    D 40 KB

    Answer

129. What size are 75% of the files smaller than?
    A 125 KB
    B 105 KB
    C 95 KB
    D 65 KB

    Answer

130. What is the inter-quartile range for the size of data files?
    A 150
    B 120
    C 100
    D 60

    Answer

Data set 14: The web-building company

The web-building company plans an aggressive programme of expansion in output and has produced the table below to summarise four scenarios for growth of revenue from sales.

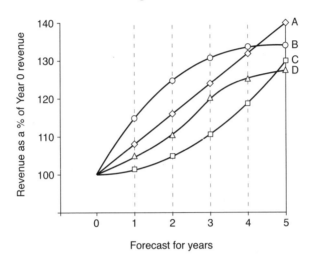

Yr 0 revenue = $26 million

131. How many years of data are detailed in the graph?
    A 21
    B 6
    C 5
    D 4

Answer ⬚

132. In Yr 3, what percentage of Yr 0 revenue is forecast in scenario D?
    A   130%
    B   122%
    C   120%
    D   110%

    Answer

133. Which scenario best fits the following figures:
    Yr 1 $30m, Yr 2 $32.5m, Yr 3 $33.8m, Yr 4 $34.5m, Yr 5 $34.7m
    A   Scenario A
    B   Scenario B
    C   Scenario C
    D   Scenario D

    Answer

134. Which scenario shows the least variation (change) over the 5 years?
    A   Scenario A
    B   Scenario B
    C   Scenario C
    D   Scenario D

    Answer

135. Assuming that revenue continues to increase by the same extent, how much more revenue as a percentage of Yr 0 revenue would you expect scenario A to realize in Yr 6?
    A   147–148%
    B   146–147%
    C   145–146%
    D   144–145%

    Answer

136. Calculate the $ forecast for revenue for scenario A in Yr 5.
    A 36.1m
    B 36.2m
    C 36.3m
    D 36.4m

    Answer ☐

137. Which of the following could help realize the planned aggressive programme of expansion in output?
    A More production facilities
    B Lowering the unit price
    C Extending the project range
    D Better distribution

    Answer ☐

138. Which is the best estimate of how much more revenue over Yr 0 scenario D will generate over Yr 1 and Yr 2 combined (take the scenario D forecast for Yr 1 to be 105%)?
    A 28m
    B 29m
    C 30m
    D 31m

    Answer ☐

139. The president of the web-building company sets as a revenue target for Yr 5 the sum of $35m. Estimate how many, if any, of the scenarios can deliver this ambitious target.
    A None of the scenarios
    B Only scenario A
    C Scenarios A and B
    D Scenarios A, B and C

    Answer ☐

140. Which scenario best fits the following figures?
    A   Yr 1 $26m, Yr 2 $27m, Yr 3 $28.5m, Yr 4 $31m, Yr 5 $34m
    B   Yr 1 $28.5, Yr 2 $30m, Yr 3 $32m, Yr 4 $34m, Yr 5 $39m
    C   Yr 1 $27m, Yr 2 $28.5m, Yr 3 $30m, Yr 4 $31.5m, Yr 5 $30m
    D   Cannot tell

Answer ☐

Twenty mini data interpretation tests

This chapter comprises 100 questions organized as 20 mini tests. Each test starts with questions at the intermediate level and concludes with questions that you can expect at the advance level. The mini tests also get harder as you progress through the chapter.

Mini tests are a great form of practice. It is far better to practise little and often and even the very busy person can find the time to sit one of these mini tests without distraction. They also help you to perfect the all-important start to a psychometric test.

A good start is important in every test but nowadays many tests are administered at a computer terminal. It is common for these tests to be what is called 'computer adaptive' and a good start is really important in a computer adaptive test. Computer adaptive means that your answers to the first few questions are used to determine the level of the next few questions. Every question is attributed a score that you cannot see. A computer adaptive test starts by presenting you with a question that carries an average score (and the average candidate is expected to get right). Answer it correctly and the next question will be one that has a higher score that, say, 40 per cent of candidates are expected to answer correctly. This adaptive process continues until you start to get questions wrong because then the program will present you with questions at the same level or with lower-scoring questions.

Making a good start in a computer adaptive test is extra important because if you get the first question wrong, the next question that the program presents you with will be low scoring and one that most candidates will get right. If you get that question right the program may still present you with a lower than average-scoring question and you will find yourself struggling to get on to sufficiently high-scoring questions to gain a score judged to be a pass. You should not read too much into this illustration but it demonstrates how it can pay dividends to practise making a good start.

In a real test every question counts, but especially resolve to get the first question right and then try your hardest to get the first five questions right (by then you should have reached questions that carry a sufficiently high score); now all you have to do is get the majority of the remaining questions right and you can expect to be awarded a winning score.

Keep practising until you consistently get all five questions right in these mini tests. Achieve this and you can take strength from the fact that you are likely to make a very good start in a real test of data interpretation.

Create a real test feel by setting yourself the personal challenge of trying to match or beat your last score each time that you take a mini test. You will need to take the challenge seriously if you are to realize this.

If you consistently get questions wrong or fail to complete the mini test within the time allowed, then identify the sorts of error you are making, go back to the warm-up chapter and revise those operations or simply practise answering the question quickly so that you improve your speed without affecting your accuracy.

Each mini test comprises one set of data and five questions that relate to it. All questions are multiple choice. Unless you are instructed otherwise, take it that each question has only one correct answer. Select the answer you judge to be correct from those suggested and write your selected answer in the answer box.

Allow yourself six minutes in which to attempt the five questions. Use as much scrap or scratch paper as you like, but do not use a calculator. Do approximate answers and eliminate suggested answers but only use straight guessing as a last resort or when time is running out.

Mini test 1: Speeding vehicles

The five bar graphs record the number of vehicles exceeding the speed limit at four locations over a five-day period. Location 1 is a residential street with a 20 mph limit, location 2 has a 30 mph limit, location 3 a 50 mph limit and location 4 (a toll road) a 70 mph limit.

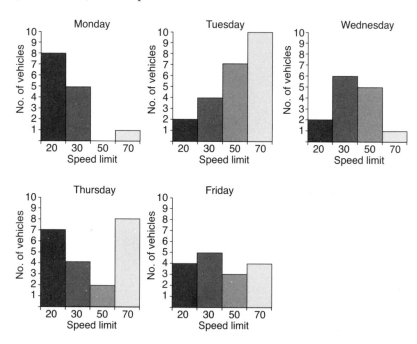

1. On what day or days were the least number of vehicles recorded as exceeding a speed limit?
    A   Monday and Wednesday
    B   Thursday and Friday
    C   Tuesday
    D   None of these

    Answer

2.   On how many days did the MAJORITY of the total number of vehicles recorded exceed the 20 and 30 mph limit combined?

A   5 days
B   4 days
C   3 days
D   2 days

Answer ☐

3.   Over the five-day period, how many vehicles exceeded the speed limit on the residential street?

A   18
B   20
C   23
D   Cannot tell

Answer ☐

4.   On Tuesday, what percentage of the total vehicles that exceeded a speed limit exceeded the 50 and 70 mph limit combined?

A   65%
B   66%
C   67%
D   68%

Answer ☐

5.   Which of the following statements are true (select more than one suggested answer as correct)?

A   Records for Friday ≥ 15
B   Records for Wednesday < 14
C   Records for Tuesday ≤ 25
D   Records for Thursday > 24

Answer ☐

Mini test 2: The mail order company

The flow diagram below illustrates the delivery options and charging policy for a US-based mail order company. Refer to the diagram to answer the questions that follow.

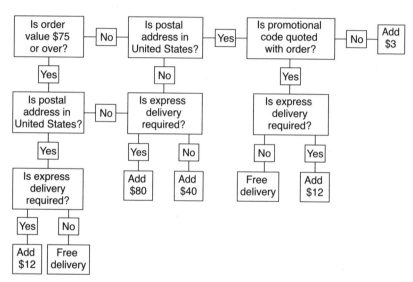

1.   How much is added to an order (without a promotional code) valued at $25 with a postal address not in the United States and not requiring express delivery?

   A $40

   B $65

   C $80

   D   None of these

   Answer ☐

2. How much less is added to an order with a US postal address that requires express delivery than an order with a non-US address that does not require express delivery if the order value is $75?
    A $68
    B $40
    C $28
    D $12

    Answer

3. How much MORE is added to an order from a non-US postal address if the order is valued at $70 and requires express delivery but does not have a promotional code, compared with an order with a US postal address with a value of $80 that does not have a promotional code and does not require express delivery?
    A $26
    B $40
    C $68
    D $80

    Answer

4. Express delivery is an option for which of the following orders (note more than one suggested answer is correct)?
    A   One with a US postal address without a promotional code and with a value under $75
    B   One with a value over $75 with a non-US postal address
    C   One with a value under $75 with a non-US postal address
    D   One with a US postal address with a promotional code and with a value over $75

    Answer

5. Which of the following are always a requirement if an order is to qualify for free delivery (note that more than one suggested answer is correct)?

    A   Value over $75
    B   A promotional code
    C   Decline express delivery
    D   A US postal address

    Answer ☐

Mini test 3: Analysis of a population by economic activity and district

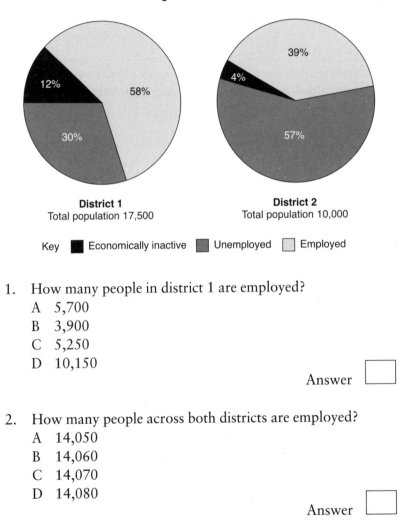

District 1
Total population 17,500

District 2
Total population 10,000

Key ■ Economically inactive ■ Unemployed □ Employed

1. How many people in district 1 are employed?
   A   5,700
   B   3,900
   C   5,250
   D   10,150

   Answer

2. How many people across both districts are employed?
   A   14,050
   B   14,060
   C   14,070
   D   14,080

   Answer

3. Are more people unemployed in district 1 or in district 2?
    A   District 1
    B   District 2
    C   They are the same

    Answer ☐

4. Express in its simplest form the ratio between economically inactive people and people not economically inactive (those unemployed or employed) in districts 1 and 2 combined.
    A   1 : 7
    B   3 : 11
    C   3 : 22
    D   1 : 10

    Answer ☐

5. What percentage of people economically inactive across both districts are resident in district 2?
    A   16%
    B   17%
    C   18%
    D   19%

    Answer ☐

Mini test 4: What young people find most and least interesting

A group of young people were presented with four issues and each asked to indicate in which they were most and least interested. All of the group completed the survey and the results are presented in the two graphs below.

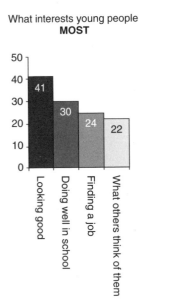

What interests young people
MOST

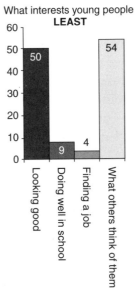

What interests young people
LEAST

1. How many young people took part in the survey?

   A   54
   B   97
   C   117
   D   234

   Answer

2. How many more young people were most interested in looking good and about what others think of them combined than doing well in school?

    A   33
    B   54
    C   76
    D   95

    Answer

3. Exactly 1/3 of the young people who took part in the survey responded to one of the four issues (ie they indicated that it was the issue that most or least interested them). Which issue was it?

    A   Looking good
    B   Doing well in school
    C   Getting a job
    D   What others think of them

    Answer

4. How many times more did young people indicate that they were most interested in finding a job compared with those who indicated that they were least interested in finding a job?

    A   ×3
    B   ×4
    C   ×5
    D   ×6

    Answer

5. What is the ratio between young people most interested in looking good and what others think of them combined to the young people most interested in doing well in school and finding a job combined?

    A   9 : 7
    B   7 : 6
    C   8 : 9
    D   6 : 5

    Answer

Mini test 5: Global sales by world regions

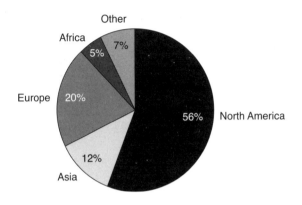

The 'Other' category comprises:

Brazil	30%
Mexico	40%
Argentina	20%

The value of the global market in 2008 (actual) was $260m. The global value (forecast) in 2009 is $500m.

1. How many times is the value of the European sales bigger than the value of sales in Africa?
   A ×4
   B ×5
   C ×6
   D ×7

   Answer [ ]

2. Express in its simplest form the ratio between the comparative sizes of the US market and the segment of the pie chart labelled Other.

    A   6 : 1
    B   7 : 1
    C   8 : 1
    D   9 : 1

    Answer ☐

3. In 2007 the US share of sales was worth $224m. What was the value of all sales that year?

    A $380m
    B $400m
    C $420m
    D $440m

    Answer ☐

4. In 2008, what was the value of sales in Argentina?

    A $3.62m
    B $3.63m
    C $3.64m
    D $3.65m

    Answer ☐

5. In 2009, the value of the European market is forecast to contract by $7m of its 2008 value. What percentage of the value of global sales in 2009 is the European market predicted to fall to?

    A   18%
    B   15%
    C   11%
    D   9%

    Answer ☐

Mini test 6: The recruitment agency

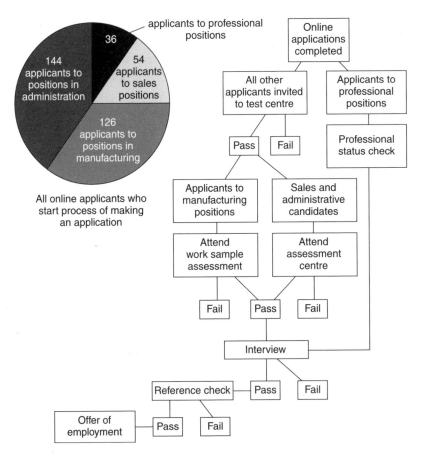

Note:
75% of online candidates to professional services complete online applications.
50% of online candidates to manufacturing, sales and administration positions complete online applications.

Percentage of remaining applicants who pass stages of the
recruitment process

Applicants to positions in	Manufacturing	Sales and administration	Professional
Pass test centre	71.5%	66%	–
Pass work sample	60%	–	–
Pass assessment centre	–	55%	–
Pass interview	75%	50%	33%
Pass reference check	60%	70%	80%

1. How many sales and administrative applicants were invited
    to attend the test centre?
    A   198
    B   244
    C   99
    D   54

    Answer ☐

2. What is the ratio between the number of online applications
    made for professional and sales positions?
    A   4 : 6
    B   5 : 6
    C   3 : 5
    D   4 : 5

    Answer ☐

3. Assuming that none were rejected at the professional status check, how many applicants to professional services failed at interview?

    A   27
    B   18
    C   9
    D   3

    Answer ☐

4. How many manufacturing candidates passed the work sample stage?

    A   63
    B   45
    C   31
    D   27

    Answer ☐

5. Half of all candidates made an offer of employment accept it and start work. If overall 1/18 of candidates who start the process of making an application are made an offer of employment, how many start work?

    A   20
    B   15
    C   10
    D   5

    Answer ☐

Mini test 7: Population growth

In 2008 the United Nations projected that by 2050 the world's population would increase by 37 per cent. That same year (2008) the US population was found to be 305 million and growing at an annual rate 0.88 per cent. The US population was projected to continue to grow until 2050 by when it would reach 439 million. In 2008 the US Census Board found that people under 18 years of age made up a quarter of the population and people 65 or more years of age represented 1/8 of the population. They also found that 80.8 per cent of the population of America lived in urban centres and the most populous states were Texas and California. These trends are expected to continue to a point when 28 per cent of the population is expected to be resident in the two states.

1. How many Americans did the Census Board find in 2008 to be aged 65 or more?
    A   38,125,000
    B   50,330,000
    C   57,187,000
    D   76,250,000

    Answer

2. How many Americans did the Census Board find lived in rural (ie non-urban) locations?
    A   246,440,000
    B   123,220,000
    C   58,560,000
    D   58,650,000

    Answer

3. Is the projected rate of growth between 2008 and 2050 in the US population:

   A   Less than the UN projected rate of increase in the world population 2008–2050

   B   Greater than the UN projected rate of increase in the world population 2008–2050

   C   Neither less nor more than the UN projected rate increase in the world population 2008–2050 but the same rate, namely 37%

   D   Cannot tell

   Answer ☐

4. How many Americans are projected to be residents of either Texas or California by 2050?

   A   85,400,000
   B   122,920,000
   C   178,400,000
   D   Cannot tell

   Answer ☐

5. If in 2050 people under 18 still make up a quarter of the population and people 65 and over still represent 1/8 of the population, then how many Americans will be aged between 18 and 64 years?

   A   297,178,000
   B   274,375,000
   C   213,869,000
   D   164,625,000

   Answer ☐

Mini test 8: Pi Corporation

Pi Corporation creates and sells intellectual products and employs a total of 54,000 workers, including a team of knowledge workers drawn from all over the world.

All immigrant knowledge workers at Pi Corporation

1. How many knowledge workers are there at Pi Corporation?
    A 270
    B 269
    C 268
    D Cannot tell

    Answer

2. Express the number of knowledge workers identified on the graph from the continent of America as a ratio to the total number of immigrant knowledge workers.
    A 1 : 6
    B 1 : 5
    C 1 : 4
    D 1 : 3

    Answer

3. What percentage of the total number of immigrant knowledge
    workers are from Africa?
    A   20%
    B   25%
    C   30%
    D   35%

    Answer

4. What proportion of the total number of immigrant knowledge
    workers are from India and the continent of Europe combined?
    A   0.4
    B   0.37
    C   0.34
    D   0.3

    Answer

5. What percentage of all workers at Pi Corporation are
    knowledge workers from China?
    A   0.5%
    B   0.4%
    C   0.05%
    D   0.04%

    Answer

Mini test 9: Worldwide.com

Worldwide.com has 3 production plants: (No 1) in Poland, (No 2) in Bangladesh and (No 3) in Mexico. Labour productivity figures are not yet available for Mexico but they are for Bangladesh (team A) and Poland (team B).

Labour productivity = output ÷ labour hours
Output = labour hours × units per hour per machine × number of machines
Capital productivity = output ÷ number of machines
Capacity utilization = output as a percentage of maximum production

Labour productivity

Team	Labour hours	Units per hour per machine
A	120	50
B	144	45

Capital productivity

Production plant	Number of machines
1	10
2	15
3	20

1.   What is the output for Bangladesh?
     A   120,000 units
     B   90,000 units
     C   82,000 units
     D   60,000 units

                                        Answer

2. What is the capital productivity of the plant in Poland?
    A   3.2
    B   6,000
    C   6,480
    D   2.4

    Answer

3. What is the labour productivity for Bangladesh?
    A   400
    B   750
    C   6,000
    D   90,000

    Answer

4. Each machine at the plant in Poland has a maximum production of 8,100 units. What is the capacity utilization at this plant?
    A   80%
    B   78%
    C   18%
    D   8%

    Answer

5. The capital productivity figure for Mexico at last arrives and is 2,760. What is the mean output for the production plants of Worldwide.com?
    A   67,000
    B   68,000
    C   71,000
    D   70,000

    Answer

Mini test 10: Number of couples celebrating their 80th wedding anniversary

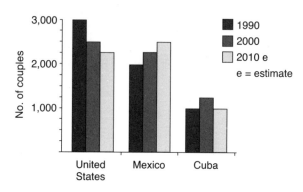

Populations

	1990	2000	2010
United States	300m	312m	e320m
Mexico	100m	105m	e115m
Cuba	12.5m	13m	e14m

1. In what year did couples marry if they celebrate their 80th wedding anniversary in 2017?
   A   1933
   B   1935
   C   1937
   D   1940

   Answer

2. In 1990, for every Cuban how many Americans were there?
    A   24
    B   26
    C   28
    D   30

    Answer ☐

3. In total (ie in the three countries combined), how many more couples celebrated their 80th wedding anniversary in 1990 than are estimated to celebrate in 2010?
    A   1,000
    B   750
    C   500
    D   250

    Answer ☐

4. In 1990, what fraction of the population of the United States had celebrated their 80th wedding anniversary?
    A   1 in 100,000
    B   1 in 75,000
    C   1 in 50,000
    D   1 in 25,000

    Answer ☐

5. In which country and in which period did the population grow by the greatest percentage?
    A   United States between 1990 and 2000
    B   Mexico between 2000 and 2010
    C   Cuba between 1990 and 2000
    D   Mexico between 1990 and 2000

    Answer ☐

Mini test 11: Employment trends by region

Latest job loss/gain by region (000)

North	+33
North East	+70
North West	+172
South	−360
South East	−270
South West	−140

Negative = loss, positive = gain

Previous total jobs by region (00,000)

North	1,8
North East	1,4
North West	2,2
South	2,4
South East	1,6
South West	2,3

1. What is the new total number of jobs for the South West?
   A 1,117,000
   B 1,600,000
   C 1,960,000
   D 2,160,000

   Answer

2. What is the net change in jobs (across all regions)? Be sure to indicate whether the change is negative or positive.
    A   −495,000
    B   +500,000
    C   −505,000
    D   +510,000

    Answer

3. In relative terms, which southern region saw the second largest variation (change) in jobs?
    A   South
    B   South East
    C   South West

    Answer

4. Which region now has the third most jobs?
    A   South
    B   South West
    C   North West
    D   North

    Answer

5. What is the new total number of jobs in the region whose job total increased by 12 per cent of the total increase in jobs?
    A   1,470,000
    B   2,370,000
    C   1,833,000
    D   2,160,000

    Answer

Mini test 12: Observations of cetaceans

Ocean-dwelling mammals (cetaceans), including dolphins and whales, have streamlined-shaped bodies so that they can move swiftly through the water in pursuit of their prey and to escape predators. They have a thick layer of fat beneath their skin which insulates them from the cold. The pie chart details the sighting of cetaceans over one season from an observation station located on the island of Flora in the Atlantic.

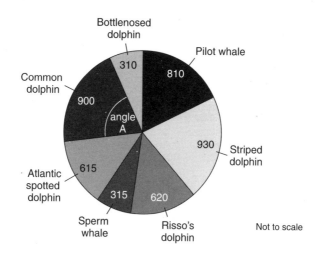

1. How many sightings of dolphins of all types are reported in the data set (excluding whales)?

   A   3,375

   B   3,376

   C   3,377

   D   3,378

   Answer

2. What is the ratio of whale to dolphin sightings?
    A   1 : 3
    B   1 : 4
    C   2 : 7
    D   3 : 29

    Answer

3. What percentage of all cetacean sightings were of sperm whales?
    A   28%
    B   17%
    C   12%
    D   7%

    Answer

4. What is the ratio between sightings of Bottlenose, Striped and
    Risso's dolphins?
    A   3 : 2 : 1
    B   2 : 3 : 2
    C   1 : 3 : 2
    D   2 : 1 : 3

    Answer

5. If the pie chart was drawn so that each sector was represented
    proportionately, what should angle a be?
    A   71°
    B   72°
    C   73°
    D   90°

    Answer

Mini test 13: Average propensity to save

Average propensity to save (APS) is a measure of a population's attitude towards saving money (the lower the APS the higher the propensity to save). In many instances APS is determined by culture. Some communities, for example in the Far East, place considerable importance on saving, while others (examples include developed Western nations) do not. These cultural differences are reflected in wide differences in the APS of populations. Take, for example, the population of the Punjab (population 5 in the table below): their APS is 0.7 and is among the highest in the world.

Population	Average saving $	Average income $
1	1,400	8,400
2	160	1,920
3	7,950	31,800
4	15,000	13,500
5	6,000	4,200
6	1,700	18,700

1. What is the APS for population 1?
   A   6
   B   7
   C   8
   D   Cannot tell

   Answer ☐

2. Which population would you estimate to place the least emphasis on the need to save?
    A   2
    B   3
    C   6
    D   Cannot tell

    Answer

3. Calculate the APS for populations 1, 2 and 5.
    A   6
    B   6.2
    C   5.8
    D   5.7

    Answer

4. If the average savings for population 6 were to increase by $2,040 (while income remained the same), what would the APS become?
    A   6
    B   5
    C   4
    D   3

    Answer

5. By how much would saving increase for population 3 if average income for that population were to increase to 39,750 while the APS remained the same?
    A $1,986
    B $1,986.5
    C $1,987
    D $1,987.5

    Answer

Mini test 14: Paper is big business

As their name suggests, Just Paper sell paper and quite a lot of it to businesses right across the United States. Their bestselling line is 'Universal White', an A4 sheet suitable for all types of photo-copier and printer. It is sold in reams of 500 sheets and there are 1,000 reams to a ton weight. Just Paper is the market leader because their prices are highly competitive and the quality of their products is high. In 2003 Just Paper's list price for a ream of Universal White was $2.00 but the company has always discounted this price for bulk purchases.

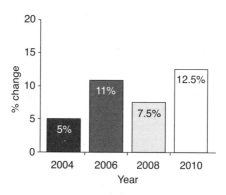

Tons sold

Year	Tons (000)
2004	58.3
2005	74.2
2006	82.4
2007	92.7
2008	93.9
2009	94.3
2010	95.5

Discounts offered on bulk purchases

Reams	% Discount
100	5
300	12.5
500	15

1. How much would you expect a customer in 2004 to pay for 100 reams of Universal White?
   A $2.10
   B $1.99
   C $210.00
   D $199.50

   Answer

2. How many more reams of Universal White did Just Paper sell in 2009 than in 2008?
   A 400,000
   B 300,000
   C 300
   D 400

   Answer

3. What was the mean annual rate of change in the percentage price of paper over the period shown?
   A 9%
   B 8%
   C 6%
   D 3%

   Answer

4. Using a straight line trend, between 2004 and 2006, which is the best estimate of Just Paper's total value of sales of Universal White in 2005 before allowing for any discount on bulk purchases?

    A $162.6m
    B $167.7m
    C $167,700
    D $167,600

    Answer

5. Without taking account of any other consideration, use a straight line trend to identify the best estimate of the percentage change in 2012.

    A   15%
    B   12.5%
    C   11.5%
    D   9%

    Answer

Mini test 15: The aged debt recovery process

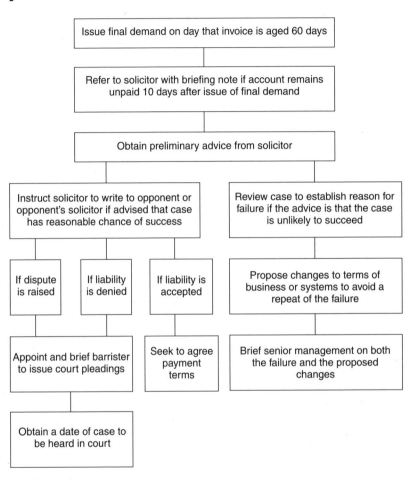

Analysis of accounts 60+ days values and outcomes

Item	Today	30 days ago	180 days ago
No. of final demands issued	210	231	126
Value of invoices to which the final demands related	$66,255	$72,880	$39,753
No. of invoices referred to solicitor	168	145	79
Value of invoices referred to solicitor	$53,004	$45,747	$24,924
No. of invoices where dispute is raised or liability denied	94	91	50
Value of disputed invoices	$29,657	$28,710	$15,775
No. of invoices where liability is admitted	12	9	6
Value of invoices where liability is denied	$3,786	$2,839	$1,893
No. of court cases pending	3,425	4,007	3,253
Value of invoices pending court cases	$1.08m	$1.26m	$1.02m

Note: average age of items when heard at court = 190 days.

1. What age is an invoice when it is referred to a solicitor?
    A   80 days
    B   70 days
    C   60 days
    D   Cannot tell

Answer ☐

2. Thirty days ago, in how many cases was the liability for the sum invoiced admitted?

   A   45

   B   44

   C   43

   D   Cannot tell

   Answer ☐

3 Which is the best estimate of the average invoice value?

   A $300

   B $305.5

   C $315.5

   D $350

   Answer ☐

4. It is expected that slightly over $1m of the value of invoices pending court cases from 30 days ago will be recovered. Which of the following percentages is the best estimate of this success rate at court?

   A   65%

   B   70%

   C   75%

   D   80%

   Answer ☐

5. One hundred and eighty (180) days ago, what percentage of invoices with the solicitor were found to be disputed or the liability denied?

   A   40%

   B   63%

   C   64%

   D   Cannot tell

   Answer ☐

Mini test 16: World population

The world has a 150m km² of land and a population density per km² of 63.

Population density

Country	Land area km²	Population
1	77,474	7,800,000
2	450,000	9,200,000
3	30,000	58,000,000

Annual population change

Country	Live births per 1,000 of population	Deaths per 1,000 of population
1	15.3	9.9
2	8	9.1
3	2.4	1.7
The rest of the world	14.1	10.1

1. Which country experiences 139,200 births a year?
    A   1
    B   2
    C   3
    D   Rest of the world

    Answer

2. Which country has a population density per km^2 closest to 100?
   A 1
   B 2
   C 3
   D Cannot tell

   Answer [   ]

3. How many more times is country 2 bigger than country 3?
   A ×13
   B ×14
   C ×15
   D ×16

   Answer [   ]

4. What fraction of the world's population lives in countries 1, 2 and 3 combined?
   A 1/100
   B 1/115
   C 1/120
   D 1/126

   Answer [   ]

5. In real terms, is country 1, 2 or 3 experiencing the fastest rate of population growth?
   A 1
   B 2
   C 3
   D Cannot tell

   Answer [   ]

Mini test 17: A survey of age and attitudes

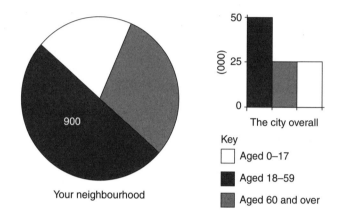

Your neighbourhood

The city overall

Key

☐ Aged 0–17

■ Aged 18–59

▨ Aged 60 and over

Note: Your neighbourhood has a population of 1,749; 1 in 3 people are aged 60 or more; 37 per cent aged 0–59 years are positive about their local community but this figure drops to 29 per cent in the 60 and older group; 1 in 9 of the 18–59 group intend to vote at the next election, but this figure rises to 1 in 5 for the 60 and over cohort. In the city overall, 1/4 are aged 60 or over; 52 per cent of people aged 0–59 years are positive about their local community but this figure drops to 41 per cent in the 60 and older group; 1 in 8 of the 18–59 group intend to vote at the next election, but this figure rises to 1 in 5 for the 60 and over cohort (the right to vote is gained at 18 years of age).

1. How many people in your neighbourhood are aged 0–17?
   A 583
   B 284
   C 266
   D Cannot tell

   Answer ☐

2. How many people in the city overall do NOT intend to vote at the next election?
   A   36,250
   B   63,500
   C   63,750
   D   64,000

   Answer ☐

3. How many people in your neighbourhood (aged 18 or more) are positive about their local community?
   A   470
   B   479
   C   450
   D   451

   Answer ☐

4. How many MORE people who live in the city but outside your neighbourhood are aged 60 or more than 0–17 years of age?
   A   634
   B   635
   C   636
   D   637

   Answer ☐

5. Which of the following is true:
   A   More people in the city overall are aged 60 or more than people between the age 0–17 years
   B   Your neighbourhood makes up less than 2% of the population of the city overall.
   C   1,483 people in your neighbourhood are old enough to vote.
   D   Fewer people in your neighbourhood 60 or more years of age plan to vote than people aged 18–59.

   Answer ☐

Mini test 18: Where there is muck there is money

Shining Products sell cleaning fluids into cut-price supermarket chains. A typical agreement with the supermarkets is signed for three years and involves Shining accepting a price drop of 5 per cent each year over the life of the contract. The contract also commits Shining to supply a minimum range of five key products in the quantities shown for the full three years of the contract.

Product number	Description	Revenue first year ($000)	* Key product required by contract
100034	Window Cleaner	$84	*
100035	Oven Cleaner	$94.8	
100036	Floor Cleaner	$202.5	*
100037	Wood Polish	$664	*
100038	Surface Cleaner	$218.75	*
100039	Air Freshener	$328	
100040	Toilet Cleaner	$237.5	*
100041	Anti Static Spray	$66.4	

Product number	Units (000)	Cost per unit year 1	Receipt per unit year 1
100034	140	$0.52	$0.60
100035	120	$0.64	$0.79
100036	750	$0.26	$0.27
100037	800	$0.79	$0.83
100038	625	$0.28	$0.35
100039	400	$0.64	$0.82
100040	950	$0.21	$0.25
100041	80	$0.77	$0.83

1. If in the first year the contract is worth $1,896,000, which of
    the following values is the best estimate of the contract's value
    in its third year?
    A $1,611,600
    B $1,691,230
    C $1,711,140
    D $1,801,200

    Answer ☐

2. By how much would revenue fall in year 1 if Shining Products
    were to discontinue lines 100035 and 100041?
    A $161,200
    B $163,200
    C $1,63,200
    D $1,642,000

    Answer ☐

3. How many, if any, of the 5 key products will Shining
    Products make a loss on in the second year of the contract if
    their costs per unit remain unchanged?
    A 0
    B 1
    C 2
    D 3

    Answer ☐

4. On which key product or products does Shining Products
    make their best margin?
    A 100034
    B 100036
    C 100037
    D 100038

    Answer ☐

5. One of Shining Products' customers is a $1 store chain which sells everything for $1 or less. Typically this store marks up goods by 280 per cent. How many of Shining Products' products could it purchase (at the value stated in the column 'receipt per unit year 1') and sell at $1 while maintaining this percentage mark-up?

    A   2
    B   3
    C   4
    D   5

                                                    Answer

Mini test 19: The reasons young people commit crime

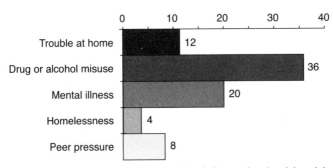

Reason given by 80 young people convicted of one crime involving violence

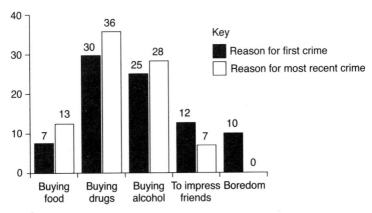

Reason given by 84 young people convicted of more than one crime involving property

1. How many crimes are detailed in the two charts?
    A   248
    B   164
    C   84
    D   80

    Answer

2. How many more young people identified buying alcohol or drugs as the reason for their most recent crime compared to their first?

    A   3

    B   6

    C   9

    D   12

    Answer

3. What fraction of recipients said that the reason they committed a crime involving violence was mental illness or homelessness?

    A   3/10

    B   5/12

    C   2/5

    D   4/9

    Answer

4. What is the best estimate of the percentage of all crimes for which the reason is cited as the misuse or purchase of alcohol or drugs?

    A   61%

    B   61.5%

    C   62%

    D   62.5%

    Answer

5. In percentage terms, how many more of the cohort of young people convicted of a crime involving violence gave as the reason drug or alcohol misuse over trouble at home?

    A   33%

    B   32%

    C   31%

    D   30%

    Answer

Mini test 20: All good things come to an end

'Mare' is a supermarket chain that has enjoyed many years of uninterrupted revenue growth and high levels of profitability (over the period shown, an average 20 per cent profit margin has been realized on the value of total sales). In 2009, however, a major supermarket chain with a reputation for low prices will open a series of stores in direct competition with each of Mare's outlets. This discovery has greatly alarmed the management team at Mare, especially given the fact that in a recent survey Mare's customers quoted value for money as the most important factor in deciding where they shop.

Value of total sales revenue

2003	2004	2005	2006	2007	2008
$29.5	$30.4	$31.3	$32.2	$33.2	$34.2

Market research in 2003 found that all of Mare's six supermarket outlets are located in residential areas with an average population of 135,000. Each outlet has 5,400 customers a day. In 2008 the most profitable lines were groceries and processed foods. Research into Mare's 'soon to arrive' competitor shows that they routinely price goods at 12 per cent below Mare's current prices.

1. On an average day in 2003, what percentage of the population
    in which a Mare outlet is located could have been expected to
    visit the store?
    A   5%
    B   4%
    C   3%
    D   Cannot tell

    Answer ☐

2. Which of the following actions would least assist Mare's
    management team in meeting the threat?
    A   An across-the-board cut of 2.5% in the price of all products
    B   The introduction of a very competitively priced range of
        everyday essential products
    C   The introduction of a membership scheme that rewarded
        customer loyalty with very low priced special offers
    D. Offering a series of 'added value' services not offered by
        the competitor, such as free home delivery, longer store
        opening hours and online shopping

    Answer ☐

3. How much more profit did Mare show in 2008 compared
    with 2003?
    A $910,000
    B $920,000
    C $930,000
    D $940,000

    Answer ☐

4. One member of the management team is concerned that groceries and processed food prices should not be cut in case it undermines customers' perception of quality. Which of the following strategies would allow Mare to introduce lower prices while avoiding the suggestion that savings have been made by reducing quality (note that more than one of the suggested answers is correct)?

    A   Adopt a pricing policy where Mare lowers all its prices but maintains a small premium over the prices of its competitor for all its groceries and processed foods lines

    B   Offer tasting opportunities in the stores so that customers can decide for themselves if quality has been compromised

    C   Introduce a money-back guarantee if a customer is not entirely happy with the quality of their purchase

    D   Cut prices only of the grocery and processed food products that the competitor does not also sell while maintaining the higher price for lines that both stores sell

    Answer

5. Mare's management team responded to the threat by cutting all 2009 prices by 9 per cent and forecast that this cut would mean that revenue in 2009 would be 10 per cent lower than the revenue figure for 2008. Much to their surprise, however, the price cut stimulated higher sales volumes and the result was that sales revenue for 2009 ended up only 3 per cent down rather than the 10 per cent forecast. How much better was the actual sales revenue for 2009 over the forecast for that year?

    A   3.42m

    B   2.89m

    C   2.394m

    D   1.026m

    Answer

Three full-length realistic data interpretation tests

This chapter comprises 90 questions organized as three realistic full-length practice tests. The tests provide a genuine test experience in terms of the question types, time allowed and the necessary sheer hard work and sustained concentration required of a real data interpretation test.

Data interpretation tests require you to extract the relevant information from tabulated and graphic sources and to reason with the figures you extract. You are expected to be entirely competent in the key mathematical operations. Even when you are allowed a calculator, a well-practised candidate will often be quicker without one and, importantly, will know if under the pressure of the test they have mis-keyed a sum. Working without a calculator also helps master the important strategies of estimation and elimination. This involves rounding up sums to convenient figures, so greatly speeding up the calculation (estimation) and looking at the suggested answers and ruling some out as incorrect (elimination). So put the calculator away and undertake this practice without one.

Remember to rely only on the information provided in the data set. If you know something about the subject then be especially careful not to bring your own knowledge or assumptions to the questions. Be sure to use only the figures and information provided to answer the questions, even if you believe those figures or information to be false.

To get an authentic test feel, stick to the time limit. Few people will finish these tests in the time allowed and even fewer will finish all the questions and get them all right. This is the case for real tests too (a test would be of rather limited use if most of the candidates correctly completed all of the questions in the time allowed). The highest-scoring candidates correctly complete the most questions. Practise not spending too long on any one question. Before undertaking a long series of calculations, check that there is not a faster way to identify the correct answer.

Take the first test and score it (allow 1 mark for each correct answer), then try to beat your score when you take test 2. Finally take test 3, and once again try to beat your previous scores. To improve your score each time you will have to take the challenge really seriously and try hard until the very end of the time allowed.

Record your scores in the boxes below:

Test 1 ☐

Test 2 ☐

Test 3 ☐

Test 1

This test comprises 30 questions and you are allowed 40 minutes in which to complete it. There are four sets of data. The first two are followed by 5 questions each and the last two are followed by 10 questions each.

All questions are multiple choice and you are required to select one of the suggested answers labelled A–D as the correct answer and record its corresponding letter of the alphabet in the answer box.

To do well in this test you will have to avoid spending too long on any one of these questions and work quickly and hard. You will also have to sustain a high level of concentration over the full 40 minutes.

You should be able to answer these questions without a calculator, but use as much scrap or scratch paper as you wish. Work without interruption.

Do not turn over the page until you are ready to begin.

Data set 1: Unit cost falls as production increases

Splash.Inc produces fabric sold in rolls of 35 metres (units) for the wholesale textile market. The production manager at Splash.Inc has produced the following table to illustrate how the unit cost of their bestselling product falls as production increases. Total costs are derived by adding fixed costs and variable costs; the fixed costs used in the calculations total $3m.

Scenario	Total cost $	Unit cost $
A	$4,500,000	$18.00
B	$5,400,000	$17.46
C	$6,477,000	$16.94
D	$7,776,000	$16.43

1. How much are the variable costs in scenario B?
    A $2,400,000
    B $1,500,000
    C $750,000
    D   Cannot tell

    Answer ☐

2. How many units are produced in scenario A?
    A   2,500,000
    B   1,250,000
    C   250,000
    D   225,000

    Answer ☐

3. How many more units are produced in scenario C compared
    to scenario A?
    A   131,000
    B   132,349
    C   136,998
    D   139,274

    Answer ☐

4. By what percentage did the total unit cost in scenario A
    increase in order to realize the unit cost reduction between
    scenarios A and B?
    A   117%
    B   119%
    C   120%
    D   121%

    Answer ☐

5. Which suggested answer would provide the best estimate of
    the unit cost if variable costs were $750,000?
    A $28 × 103% = new unit price
    B $18 × 97% = new unit price
    C   New unit cost × 103% = $18
    D   New unit cost × 97% = $18

    Answer ☐

Data set 2: Australia and Canada

Australia and Canada are both resource producers (exporting
commodities such as ores and grain). Both economies boomed for
most of the first decade of the millennium and suffered capacity
constraints where they simply could not fulfil demand. The effect
on both economies was inflation, normally addressed through
increases in the benchmark lending rate. But when it comes to
lending rates during the period of boom, the two economies could
not have been more different.

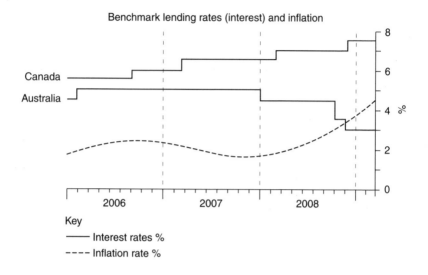

Benchmark lending rates (interest) and inflation

Key
—— Interest rates %
---- Inflation rate %

Annual value of exports ($m)

Australia	Canada	Australia	Canada	
420.402	252.241	485.7968	210.201	Iron ore
354.366	354.062	366.448	314.721	Coal
41.677	357.840	58.3478	286.272	Wheat
12.009	472.082	14.956	377.665	Timber
2006	2006	2007	2007	

6. How much higher were benchmark rates in Canada than
    Australia at the close of 2007?
    A   1%
    B   1.5%
    C   2%
    D   2.5%

                                              Answer ☐

7. In percentage terms, how much did the value of Australian exports of wheat increase between 2006/2007 (the value increased by $16,577,800)?

    A   45%
    B   40%
    C   38%
    D   35%

    Answer

8. Which statement is NOT true of the extent to which the two countries' benchmark rates changed:

    A   The benchmark rates in the two countries were closest during 2006.
    B   Over the period shown, both countries changed their rates four times.
    C   The difference between the rates in the two countries varied from 0.5 to 4.5 percentage points.
    D   At the end of 2008 Australia's rate was 3% above the inflation rate while Canada's was 1.5% below inflation.

    Answer

9. In 2006 Canada's export of timber was valued at:

    A   Twice the value of its iron ore exports
    B   1/3 more than the worth of its coal exports
    C   More than the value of its wheat exports in both 2006 and 2007 combined
    D   None of the suggested answers are correct

    Answer

10. By what percentage did Australia's combined iron ore and coal exports increase between 2006 and 2007?

A   10%

B   8%

C   6%

D   5%

Answer

Data set 3: International literacy rates 2010

Internationally accepted definitions of literacy

Level 1	Poor literacy skills
Level 2	A capacity to deal only with simple, clear material involving uncomplicated tasks
Level 3	Adequate to cope with the demands of everyday life and work in an advanced society

Level 3 is considered to be the level required for coping with the increasing skill demands of the emerging knowledge and information economy. Competence at or above level 3 is associated with a number of positive outcomes, including better health, economic success, civic participation and opportunities for learning new skills.

Findings of a study into levels of literacy 2010

Sample	Location	Sample size	% that FAILED to reach level 3*
1	Asia	229m	62
2	Europe	46m	49
3	Africa	148m	56.5

*Note
*1. Asia: female literacy rates are 16 percentage points below the male rate and half the sample were women.
*2. Africa: the literacy rate of adults living in rural locations is 27 percentage points behind their urban counterparts; 111m of the sample lived in an urban location.

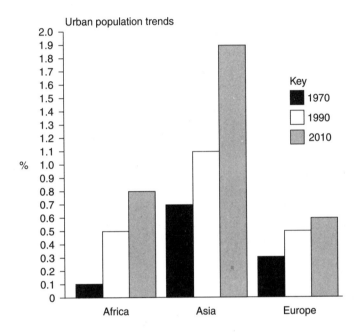

Urban population trends

Rates of literacy (level 3) by gender

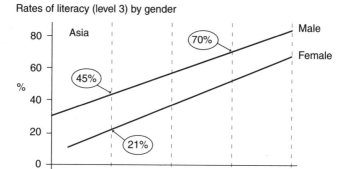

Rates of literacy (level 3) by rural/urban residency

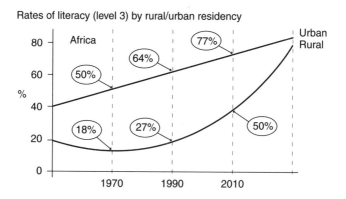

11. In 2010, what fraction of the population in sample 3 live in rural locations?

A   1/4

B   2/3

C   1/3

D   3/4

Answer

12. When did the size of Africa's urban population overtake Europe's?
   A   It hasn't yet
   B   Before 1970
   C   Between 1970 and 1990
   D   Between 1990 and 2010

   Answer

13. The percentage of women in sample 1 who FAILED to reach level 3 is:
   A   46%
   B   54%
   C   21%
   D   16%

   Answer

14. Which is the best estimate of the ratio between European and Asian participants in the survey?
   A   1 : 6
   B   2 : 7
   C   1 : 5
   D   1 : 4

   Answer

15. In 2010, how many in sample 2 REACHED level 3?
   A   23.46 million
   B   23.04 million
   C   22.83 million
   D   22.54 million

   Answer

16. By what magnitude did the urban population of the three continents (Africa, Asia and Europe) grow between 1970 and 2010?
    A ×2
    B ×2.5
    C ×3
    D ×.5

    Answer

17. In Asia, by how many percentage points did the literacy gap between men and women narrow between 1970 and 2010?
    A 8
    B 7
    C 6
    D 5

    Answer

18. In 2010, how many women in sample 1 REACHED level 3?
    A Just over 50 million
    B Just under 60 million
    C Just over 60 million
    D Just over 70 million

    Answer

19. In 1990, how many urban Africans were literate to level 3?
    A 180 million
    B 320 million
    C 135 million
    D Cannot tell

    Answer

20. Which group is the most populous?
   A Individuals in sample 2 who reached level 3
   B People in sample 1 who reached level 3
   C Women from sample 1
   D Urban dwellers in sample 3

Answer ☐

Data set 4: Royal Tea

Market research findings relating to 'Royal Tea'

Market A	Market B
Competitor brands are winning Royal Tea's market share	Market leading brand
Price-sensitive market	Sold at a premium price
Customers base buy decision almost entirely on price	High level of customer loyalty (low level of brand switching)
Brand is sold at modest premium over competitors	Customers perceive higher price to imply higher quality

Value of total sales of Royal Tea (000)

Market A	$120	$121	$115	$119
Market B	$20	$19	$18	$19
	2002	2004	2006	2008

21. What is the value of sales in market B for the period 2002–2006?

A $390,000

B $39,000

C $3,900

D   Cannot tell

Answer

22. Sales in market A in 2007 were at the mean value of the figures for that market in 2006 and 2008. What was the value of sales that year?

A $116,000

B $117,000

C $118,000

D   Cannot tell

Answer

23. How many times greater are the figures for market A than the figures for market B?

A   ×6

B   ×6.25

C   ×6.5

D   ×6.75

Answer

24. Which measure would NOT help sales in market B?

A   Lower the price

B   Increase marketing

C   Increase the price by a small percentage

D   Cannot tell

Answer

25. Sales for market B were 15% better in 2007 than 2006. What was the value of sales on that market that year?

    A 19,200
    B 19,900
    C 20,700
    D 21,200

    Answer

26. Which conclusion in the findings of the market research seems not to be supported by the sales figures?

    A Market-leading brand – market B
    B Brand is sold at modest premium over competitors – market A
    C Competitor brands are winning Royal Tea's market share – market A
    D High level of customer loyalty (low level of brand switching) – market B

    Answer

27. Sales for both markets totalled a disappointing 119,000 for 2003 and were earned at the same ratio between markets A and B as in 2002. What was the value of market A that year?

    A $102,000
    B $103,000
    C $104,000
    D $105,000

    Answer

28. By how much did sales values fall in market A and B combined between 2004 and 2006?

    A $17,000
    B $7,000
    C $70,000
    D Cannot tell

    Answer

29. If the value of sales for the two markets combined in 2002 represented 5% of global sales for the Royal Tea brand, what was the value of global sales that year?

A $2,800,000

B $2,300,000

C $1,800,000

D   Cannot tell

Answer

30. In market B the average pack of Royal Tea costs $3.80 and at this price the profit per pack is $0.57. Use this data to calculate how much profit was made in market B in 2002.

A $2,250

B $2,750

C $3,000

D   Cannot tell

Answer

End of test

Test 2

This test comprises 30 questions and you are allowed 40 minutes in which to complete it. There are five sets of data. The first four are followed by 5 questions while the last set is followed by 10 questions.

All questions are multiple choice and you are required to select one of the suggested answers labelled A–D as the correct answer and record its corresponding letter of the alphabet in the answer box.

To do well in this test you will have to avoid spending too long on any one of these questions and work quickly and hard. You will also have to sustain a high level of concentration over the full 40 minutes.

You should be able to answer these questions without a calculator. Work without interruption.

Do not turn over the page until you are ready to begin.

Data set 1: Languages of the world

There are 3,800 known languages spoken worldwide; 1/7 are expected to die out over the next 40 years and 72.5% are predicted to die out in the next 100 years. As a first language 2/7 of the world's population speak the seven most widely spoken languages and a further 1.7 billion speak one of the seven languages as a second language.

Most widely spoken languages	No. of first-language speakers (millions)
English	1,386
Chinese	1,000
Spanish	280
Russian	270
French	220
Portuguese	160
Arabic	140

1. How many speakers of the 7 most widely spoken languages are there (spoken as either first or second language)?
    A   5.223 billion
    B   5.116 billion
    C   5.156 billion
    D   5.215 billion

    Answer [   ]

2. Which suggested answer most closely represents the fraction of first-language speakers of the 7 most widely spoken languages that speak Spanish or French?
    A   1/10th
    B   1/7th
    C   1/6th
    D   1/5th

    Answer

3. How many speakers are there currently of the languages predicted to die out?
    A   7.6 billion
    B   5.2 billion
    C   3.8 billion
    D   Cannot tell

    Answer

4. How many languages are expected to die out over the next 100 years?
    A   3,800
    B   3,455
    C   2,655
    D   2,755

    Answer

5. Which suggested answer is the closest estimate of the proportion of the world's population who speak Chinese as a first language?
    A   1 in 12
    B   1 in 10
    C   1 in 8
    D   1 in 6

    Answer

Data set 2: Bluefin tuna

In the Atlantic there are two distinct bluefin tuna stocks, one that breeds in the Gulf of Mexico and the other in the Mediterranean. While the fish breed in waters 6,000 kilometres apart, they feed in the common oceanic waters of the Atlantic. Recently two adult bluefin tuna were caught off the southwest coast of Ireland (in the northwest Atlantic) and were tagged and released unharmed. The tags were tracking devices and the scientists involved watched with fascination as the two fish swam in opposite directions. One of the fish crossed the Atlantic and ended up off the coast of Florida, travelling over 5,000 km; the other stayed on the eastern side of the Atlantic and eventually moved into the Mediterranean.

In 1995 and because of the common feeding ground, the organization charged with responsibility for the management of the Atlantic and Mediterranean tuna fisheries set a single catch quota of 30,000 tonnes that year, which decreased by 1,500 tonnes a year until 2010. Unfortunately, there is a thriving market for illegally caught bluefin tuna and the collection of records of tonnes of bluefin sold at fish markets (see Tables A and B) are monitored to check that sales of bluefin do not exceed quotas. The most recent science in 2009 suggests that despite 14 years of quotas the bluefin stock is seriously depleted and the scientists recommend that the 2011 quota should be half that of 2010.

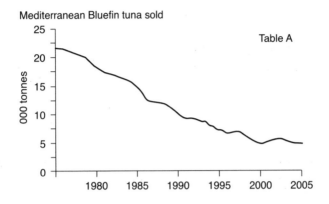

Mediterranean Bluefin tuna sold

Table A

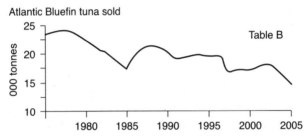

Atlantic Bluefin tuna sold

Table B

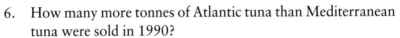

6. How many more tonnes of Atlantic tuna than Mediterranean
    tuna were sold in 1990?
    A   20,000
    B   15,000
    C   10,000
    D   5,000

    Answer

7. What was the catch quota for 2002?
    A   21,000
    B   19,500
    C   18,000
    D   16,500

    Answer

8. Did sales of bluefin exceed the quota for 2000 and, if so, by
    how much?
    A   Tonnes sold were the same as quotas
    B   Sales were 3,000 tonnes above quotas
    C   Sales were 2,000 tonnes above quotas
    D   Sales were 1,000 tonnes above quotas

    Answer [   ]

9. If the quota was to continue to be cut by 1,500 tonnes a year,
    in what year would no catch at all be allowed?
    A   2013
    B   2014
    C   2015
    D   2016

    Answer [   ]

10. How much would the Atlantic fleet's share of the quota be in
    2011 if that year's quota is to be divided between the Atlantic
    and Mediterranean fleets in the ratio 2 : 1?
    A   3,750 tonnes
    B   2,500 tonnes
    C   2,000 tonnes
    D   1,250 tonnes

    Answer [   ]

Data set 3: Hourly and weekly earnings

Average hourly earning of production workers ($)

Yr	Jan	Feb	Mar	Apr	May	Jun	Jul	Aug	Sep	Oct	Nov	Dec
1998	12.75	12.77	12.83	12.90	12.92	12.94	12.96	13.0	13.01	13.03	13.06	13.08
1999	13.13	13.16	13.19	13.24	13.27	13.32	13.39	13.45	13.50	13.56	13.60	13.62
2000	13.66	13.69	13.75	13.82	13.90	13.93	13.97	14.00	14.08	14.13	14.20	14.28
2001	14.34	14.36	14.40	14.43	14.48	14.51	14.54	14.58	14.63	14.65	14.69	14.70
2002	14.79	14.87	15.06	15.28	15.41	15.50	15.59	15.68	15.90	16.10	16.18	16.27

Average hourly earning of retail assistants ($)

Yr	Jan	Feb	Mar	Apr	May	Jun	Jul	Aug	Sep	Oct	Nov	Dec
1998	8.00	8.00	8.00	8.00	8.00	8.00	11.5	11.5	8.00	8.00	8.00	13.0
1999	8.53	8.53	8.53	8.53	8.53	8.53	8.02	8.02	8.30	8.53	8.53	13.52
2000	8.96	8.96	8.96	8.96	8.96	8.96	8.51	8.51	8.75	8.96	8.96	14.20
2001	9.32	9.32	9.32	9.32	9.32	9.32	8.85	8.85	9.08	9.32	9.32	14.63
2002	9.51	9.51	9.51	9.51	9.51	9.51	9.03	9.03	9.28	9.51	9.51	15.21

Average working week for production workers and retail assistants

	Production workers	Retail assistants
1998	39.3	47.5
1999	40.4	47.5
2000	39.0	48.9
2001	41.0	49.1
2002	40.0	43.7

11. By how much in percentage terms did retail assistants'
December average hourly earnings increase over the 5-year
period described?
   A   15%
   B   17%
   C   115%
   D   117%

   Answer

12. How much did the average production worker earn a week
in March 2001?
   A $382.12
   B $588.76
   C $590.40
   D   Cannot tell

   Answer

13. By what percentage did the average working week decrease for retail assistants in 2002 compared with 1998?

    A   5%
    B   6%
    C   7%
    D   8%

    Answer

14. What was the average hourly rate for retail assistants during 1998?

    A $8.00
    B $8.50
    C $9.00
    D $9.50

    Answer

15. How much more a week did the average production worker earn in June 2002 than in August 2000?

    A $74
    B $75
    C $76
    D $77

    Answer

Data set 4: Recorded street crimes

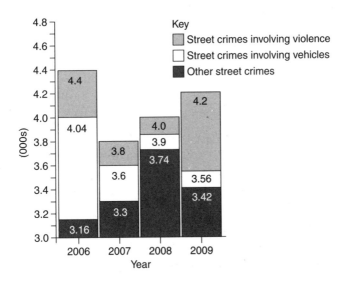

16. Assuming that the trend since 2007 continues, forecast the level of street crimes in 2010 in order to identify which of the following is correct:

    A In 2010 the peak of 2006 in street crimes will be exceeded
    B 2010 will match 2006 in terms of the level of street crime recorded
    C The level of street crime in 2010 will remain below the record set in 2006.

    Answer

17. How many street crimes are recorded for 2009?
    A 11,180
    B 5,200
    C 4,600
    D 4,200

    Answer

18. How many street crimes recorded in 2007 did not involve vehicles?

A 3,000
B 3,300
C 3,500
D 3,800

Answer [ ]

19. Which of the following statements is true?

A More crimes involving vehicles were recorded in 2009 than in 2008
B Fewer crimes involving vehicles were recorded in 2009 than in 2008
C The same number of crimes involving vehicles was recorded in 2009 as in 2008.
D None of the above are true

Answer [ ]

20. In 2006, what percentage of recorded street crimes involved vehicles?

A 17%
B 18%
C 19%
D 20%

Answer [ ]

Data set 5: Q.com

Q.com has an annual international wage bill of $42 million and an additional annual personal development budget of $1,260,000. Q.com's 2,000 employees can select to attend personal development courses to a maximum value of 5 per cent of the average salary. They may choose from the following courses:

Public speaking *	$150	2 days
Effective e-mails	$475	1 day
Demonstrating leadership**	$350	3 days
Closing a sale*	$150	1 day
Dealing with conflict	$475	1 day
Personal safety	$150	1 day

Notes

Employees can attend any course only once.

* These courses are open only to staff in sales positions.

** This course is open only to staff in managerial positions.

89% of Q.com's staff are based in the United States.

60% are in sales positions.

21. How much would it cost to attend all 6 courses?

    A $1,750

    B $1,700

    C $1650

    D $1,600

    Answer ☐

22. What is the maximum number of Q.com's staff who could attend the public-speaking course?

    A 2,000

    B 1,700

    C 1,400

    D 1,200

    Answer ☐

23. What percentage of the total wage bill at Q.com does the personal development budget represent?
   A   4%
   B   3%
   C   2%
   D   1%

   Answer ☐

24. What is the average salary at Q.com?
   A $19,000
   B $20,000
   C $21,000
   D $22,000

   Answer ☐

25. What is 5% of the average salary at Q.com?
   A $1,050
   B $1,100
   C $1,150
   D $1,200

   Answer ☐

26. What would be the total cost if 90% of staff in sales positions went on the 'closing a sale' course?
   A $160,000
   B $161,000
   C $162,000
   D $163,000

   Answer ☐

27. What is the maximum number of courses an employee who is neither a manager nor in a sales position can follow?

    A   1
    B   2
    C   3
    D   4

    Answer

28. How many of Q.com's staff are not based in the United States?

    A   1,780
    B   1,560
    C   560
    D   220

    Answer

29. What is the maximum number of courses that someone in a sales position can attend?

    A   1
    B   2
    C   3
    D   4

    Answer

30. What is the maximum amount of their personal development budget that a manager can spend?

    A $975
    B $1,000
    C $1,025
    D $1,125

    Answer

End of test

Test 3

This test comprises 30 questions and you are allowed 40 minutes in which to complete it. There are six sets of data and each is followed by five questions.

All questions are multiple choice. You are required to select one of the suggested answers labelled A–D as the correct answer and record its corresponding letter of the alphabet in the answer box.

To do well in this test you will have to avoid spending too long on any one of these questions and work quickly and hard. You will also have to sustain a high level of concentration over the full 40 minutes.

Use as much scrap or scratch paper as you like, but you should be able to answer these questions without a calculator. Work without interruption.

Do not turn over the page until you are ready to begin.

Data set 1: Dollar millionaires

These are people with a net wealth of more than $1 million, excluding the value of primary residence and consumables. The number of millionaires around the world reached 10¼ million last year, up 6 per cent from a year ago. Most of the newcomers were from China, India and Brazil. There are reportedly over 80,000 dollar millionaires in India (the second-fastest growth in the world behind Singapore). China has surpassed France and now stands fifth around the world for the number of its residents who qualify. China is reported to have about 427,000, more than France's 400,000.

The lowest per capita income

Per capita income means how much every individual would receive in monetary terms if their country's yearly income was to be divided equally among everyone living there.

Per capita income 2009

Mozambique	$81
Ethiopia	$123
Tanzania	$155
Somalia	$168
Nepal	$179

Population

Mozambique	21⅓ million
Ethiopia	79 million
Tanzania	40½ million
Somalia	8½ million
Nepal	28 million

1. How many dollar millionaires were there a year ago?
   A   9,635,000
   B   9,423,500
   C   9,400,000
   D   Cannot tell

   Answer

2 Which is the best estimate of the fraction of the world's dollar millionaires from China?
   A   1/26
   B   1/25
   C   1/24
   D   1/23

   Answer

3. Which of the countries listed has a yearly income closest to 5 billion?
   A   Mozambique
   B   Ethiopia
   C   Tanzania
   D   Somalia
   E   Nepal

   Answer

4. Which of the following statements can you establish from the data set as true?
   A   France is sixth in the league table of dollar millionaires.
   B   There are very few dollar millionaires in Ethiopia.
   C   The combined assets of the Chinese dollar millionaires are $427 million.
   D   Mozambique has the second-lowest yearly income.

   Answer

5. How much would have to be collected from each of the French millionaires if that country's $36 billion fiscal deficit was to be wiped out?

    A $990,000
    B $900,000
    C $600,000
    D $3,000,000

    Answer

Data set 2: Cibo

The owner of the restaurant chain Cibo knows that he cannot expect to see every dining place taken in every one of his nine restaurants at both lunch and dinner on very many occasions. In fact he is very pleased that over the last four months he has realized an average 68 per cent of the maximum capacity (up on the previous three-month figure of 62 per cent). He is also heartened by the fact that the average spend per customer has increased by 6 per cent on the previous three-month figure of $20. On the cost side, however, he is concerned that the extra pressure put on the kitchen by more customers and the higher expectations of the customers who pay more has meant that this period each restaurant has seen an average of almost four customers a week returning a meal as unsatisfactory, an increase on the last period of 30 per cent. He resolves to offer a full refund to every customer who returns a meal as unsatisfactory.

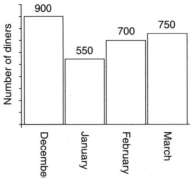

Average number of diners at a Cibo
restaurant over a 4-month period

6. How much has the average spend of each customer risen by?
   A $1.1
   B $1.2
   C $1.3
   D $1.4

   Answer ⬚

7. How much were the total takings in January?
   A $106,000
   B $104,940
   C $103,500
   D $103,000

   Answer ⬚

8. Based on the new level of business, how much should the
   owner budget for refunding returned meals each week?
   A $920
   B $763.2
   C $720
   D $80

   Answer ⬚

9. In an average week over the 4-month period shown (16
   weeks), what was the probability of a meal being returned?
   A   0.00551
   B   0.005
   C   0.0025
   D   0.000133

   Answer

10. How many customers would there have been had every
    dining place been taken at both lunch and dinner in the Cibo
    chain over the 4-month period shown?
    A   4,412
    B   Around 35,000
    C   Close to 40,000
    D   Cannot tell

    Answer

Data set 3: Life expectancy for the years 35–41 (data dated 2009)

Male age years	Probability of death within one year	Number of survivors out of 100,000 born	Average number of years remaining*
35	0.001662	96,454	41.89
36	0.001782	96,294	40.96
37	0.001918	96,122	40.04
38	0.002068	95,938	39.11
39	0.002235	95,740	38.19
40	0.002420	95,526	37.28
41	0.002629	95,294	36.36

* if the probability of death remains consistent for the remainder
of their lives.

Two most frequent causes of male death aged 0–41

Cancer of any type	8%
Heart attack from any cause	6.8%

Five most frequent causes of death 35–41

Cancer of any type	11%
Heart attack from any cause	9%
Liver disease caused by use of alcohol	8.4%
Mental and behavioural disorders	2.6%
Intentional self-harm	4.1%

11. What percentage of the original 100,000 is predicted to die over the 7-year period (35–41 years)?
    A   11.6%
    B   11.2%
    C   1.2%
    D   1.16%

    Answer

12. In what year was someone who celebrated their 35th birthday in 2009 born?
    A   1974
    B   1975
    C   1976
    D   1977

    Answer

13. How many deaths by 35 years of age are expected to be attributable to cancer of any kind?
A   400
B   284
C   274
D   264

Answer ☐

14. How many lives would be saved if all predicted deaths from intentional self-harm and liver disease caused by alcohol between the age of 35 and 41 were prevented?
A   147
B   146
C   145
D   144

Answer ☐

15. To calculate the number of survivors out of the 100,000 born for the 42-year row of the table, you must:
A   First obtain figures not provided in the table
B   Multiply 95,294 × 0.002629 and subtract the total from 95,294
C   Multiply 95,294 × 0.002629

Answer ☐

Data set 4: The Bank of Granite

The depositor base of the Bank of Granite is growing at a rate of 20,000 new accounts a week, with an average deposit of $13,000. The bank's loan margin – the difference between the interest it pays depositors and the interest it collects from borrowers – is currently 2.5 per cent annually, a full half percentage point over the industry mean.

How annual borrower rate is calculated

2008 Depositor rate = 6.170%
Loan Margin = 2.50%
2008 Borrower rate: 6.170 + 2.50 (Margin) = 8.67%*

---

* Note that the bank rounds the rate to the nearest 1/8%.

The bank is one of world's most successful. In 2008 it announced pre-tax profits of $4.2 billon and forecasts after-tax profits of $2.646 billion.

16. What would the actual borrower rate be in the example of how the borrower rate is calculated?
    A   8.75%
    B   8.67%
    C   8.625%
    D   8.875%

    Answer ☐

17. What % decrease in its 2008 pre-tax profits has the Bank of Granite allowed for in its forecast of $2.646 billion of after-tax profit?
    A   37%
    B   39%
    C   60%
    D   63%

    Answer ☐

18. How much is deposited in new accounts each week?
    A $2.6 million
    B $26 million
    C $52 million
    D $260 million

    Answer ☐

19. If in 2009 the bank was to slash its depositor rate to 1.92%
   and adopt the industry mean for its loan margin (2%), what
   would be the new borrowing rate?
   A   3.75%
   B   3.875%
   C   3.92%
   D   4%

   Answer ☐

20. If in 2008 a borrower transferred his loan of $10,000 to a
   lender offering a rate of 8.125%, how much interest would
   he save over 12 months?
   A $400
   B $86.2
   C $50
   D $40

   Answer ☐

Data set 5: Inflation in the cost of essentials

Over the winter of 2007 oil and gas wholesale price hit record
highs. Fuel oil prices rose 31.2 per cent and the increase in gas
wholesale prices meant that households on average paid $300
more a year for their domestic gas.

At the same time the price of staple foods (foods we have to buy)
increased by alarming amounts. All fruit and vegetables, for
example bananas, rose in price by a third. Dairy products, for
example butter, rose by two-thirds (a block of butter rose to $1.85)
and rice and pasta prices doubled.

% Increase in staples winter 2007

Cereals	+50%
Meat and fish	+59.6%
Dairy products	+>66.6%
Fruit and veg.	+>33.3%
Fuel oil	+31.2%

Wholesale gas prices

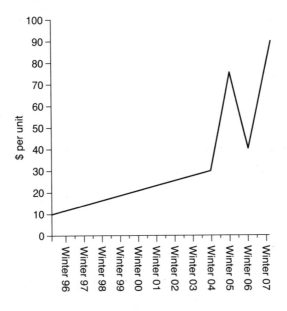

Note that for every 9% point increase in the price of wholesale gas prices, domestic bills go up 1%.

21. After the increase, how much did a family have to pay for a 500g pack of dried pasta if the previous price had been 37 cents?
    A   74 cents
    B   70 cents
    C   55.5 cents
    D   50 cents

    Answer ☐

22. How great in percentage terms was the increase in wholesale gas prices between the winters of 2006 and 2007?
    A   144%
    B   175%
    C   200%
    D   225%

    Answer ☐

23. What was the price of a block of butter prior to the increase?
    A $1.01
    B $1.11
    C $1.15
    D $1.18

    Answer ☐

24. What is the best estimate of the mean percentage increase in the five staples listed?
    A   48.14%
    B   49.23%
    C   50%
    D   Cannot tell

    Answer ☐

25. How much was the average domestic gas bill after the $300 increase?

A $1,200
B $1,350
C $1,500
D $1,650

Answer [   ]

Data set 6: Body Mass Index (BMI)

BMI classifications

Underweight = < 18.9
Normal weight = 19–24.9
Overweight = 25–29.9

The prevalence of obesity (BMI ≥ 30) continues to be a health concern in the developed nations. Data from a region in the UK in 2008 found that among adult men the prevalence of obesity was 31.1% (28.6% overweight). The individuals were followed up the following year and the 2009 figures show a change to 33.3% (30.2% overweight). Among adult women the prevalence of obesity in 2008 was 33.3% (30.5% overweight), 2009 35.3% (32.1% overweight). Its prevalence among children and adolescents in 2008 aged 2–19 years was found to be 16.3% (32.5% overweight). No figures are available for 2009. The sample involved 5,000 men, 6,000 women and 4,000 children and adolescents.

BMI Calculations for adults

Height in inches	Body weight in pounds															
	90	95	100	105	110	115	120	125	130	135	140	145	150	155	160	165
58	90	95	100	105	110	115	120	125	130	135	140	145	150	155	160	165
59	94	99	104	109	114	119	124	129	134	139	144	149	154	159	164	169
60	98	103	108	113	118	123	128	133	138	143	148	153	158	163	168	173
61	102	107	112	117	122	127	132	137	142	147	152	157	162	167	172	177
62	106	111	116	121	126	131	136	141	146	151	156	161	166	171	176	181
63	110	115	120	125	130	135	140	145	150	155	160	165	170	175	180	185
64	114	119	124	129	134	139	144	149	154	159	164	169	174	179	184	189
65	118	123	128	133	138	143	148	153	158	163	168	173	178	183	188	193
66	122	127	132	137	142	147	152	157	162	167	172	177	182	187	192	197
67	126	131	136	141	146	151	156	161	166	171	176	181	186	191	196	201
68	130	135	140	145	150	155	160	165	170	175	180	185	190	195	200	205
69	134	139	144	149	154	159	164	169	174	179	184	189	194	199	204	209
70	138	143	148	153	158	163	168	173	178	183	188	193	198	203	208	213
71	142	147	152	157	162	167	172	177	182	187	192	197	202	207	212	217
72	146	151	156	161	166	171	176	181	186	191	196	201	206	211	216	221
73	150	155	160	165	170	175	180	185	190	195	200	205	210	215	220	225
BM1→	20	21	22	23	24	25	26	27	28	29	30	31	32	33	34	35

Average height Western developed nations

All males 20–74 years	175.26 cm
All females 20–74 years	162.56 cm

Metric/imperial conversions

1 cm = 0.03937 inches
1 inch = 2.54 cm
1 pound = 0.453 kilograms
1 kilogram = 2.204 pounds

26. How much more can a 6′ tall man weigh compared to a man who is 5′9″ tall before he is classified as overweight?

    A   12 lb
    B   11 lb
    C   10 lb
    D   9lb

Answer ☐

27. How tall is the average female in feet and inches?

    A   5′6″
    B   5′4″
    C   5′3″
    D   5′2″

Answer ☐

28. How many overweight children or adolescents took part in the survey?

    A   1,150
    B   1,200
    C   1,250
    D   1,300

Answer ☐

29. How many pounds must a woman 5′6″ tall and weighing
187 lb lose in order to avoid the classification of obese?
   A   14 lb
   B   15 lb
   C   16 lb
   D   17 lb

   Answer ☐

30. What would be the BMI of a man of average height if he
weighed 67.6 kilograms?
   A   23
   B   24
   C   25
   D   26

   Answer ☐

End of test

Answers and detailed explanations

Chapter 2: One hundred and forty warm-up data interpretation questions

Data set 1

1. Answer D, 31

In every test, scratch or scrap paper is provided and this sort of question is so much easier to answer if you construct a table and enter the given information. Below is a table representing the various categories and completed with the information given in the passage and additional information.

	Number of guests	Accommodation only	Half board	Full board
2-day package	17			
5-day package		16	3	
Total guests that night	48	21		20

Explanation: We are told that there are 48 guests, 17 of whom are on the two-day package. To find the number of guests on the five-day package we simple subtract 17 from 48 to arrive at 31.

2.   Answer A, 12

Explanation: From the previous question we established that 31 guests were staying on the five-day package and we are told that 16 had opted for accommodation only and a further 3 for half board. We can calculate from this that 19 opted for accommodation only or half board and that the remaining 12 chose full board.

3.   Answer A, 5

Explanation: Using point 1 of the additional information and the information contained in the original set, we know that of the 21 people who selected accommodation only, 16 were on the five-day package, which leaves 5 on the two-day package who opted for accommodation only.

4.   Answer B, 8

Explanation: We are informed that 12 people on the five-day package selected full board and that a total of 20 guests were full board. This means that 8 people on the two-day package selected full board.

5.   Answer C, 7

Explanation: We are told that there were a total of 48 guests and that 20 were on full board. This must mean that the remaining 7 guests were half board.

6.   Answer C, 4

Explanation: In the last question it was established that a total of 7 guests were half board and we are told that 3 on the five-day package are half board. We can calculate therefore that 4 (7 – 3) of the guests on the two-day package are half board.

7.   Answer D, On the two-day package half as many people are on half board compared to full board

Explanation: On the two-day package 4 people are on half board and 8 on full board (on the five-day package 3 are on half board and 12 on full board). This means that the only true statement is D.

8.   Answer B, 9

Explanation: We have previously calculated that on the two-day package 5 people are on accommodation only and 4 are on half board. This gives us a total of 9.

9.   Answer A, Accommodation only on the five-day package

Explanation: 16 of the total number of guests opted for accommodation only on the five-day package; the next most popular option was the 12 guests who opted for full board on the five-day package.

10. Answer D, 1/4

Explanation: The total number of guests is 48 and 12 of these opted for full board on the five-day package; 12 as a fraction of 48 cancels down to 1/4.

Data set 2

11. Answer C, 20

Explanation: The survey found that 55 walk and 35 travel by bus. The difference is 20.

12. Answer D, 19

Explanation: The total who travel by either bus or car = (35 + 18) = 53; to find how many more cycled, calculate 72 − 53 = 19.

13. Answer A, 180

Explanation: The total number of responses represented is established by adding the responses to each category (55 + 35 + 18 + 72 = 180).

14. Answer A, Cycle and car; and C, Walk and bus

Explanation: You got this right only if you answered A and C (rather than A or C) as both the sum of (cycle and car) and (walk and bus) total 90 or half of the total responses represented in the survey.

15. Answer D, 2°

Explanation: There are a total of 360 degrees in the pie and the survey comprises 180 responses, so (360 ÷ 180 = 2); each response is represented by 2 degrees of arc in the pie.

16. Answer C, 1 : 4

Explanation: The number of responses for car is 18 while the number for cycle is 72. This gives us the ratio of 18 : 72 which simplifies to 1 : 4 (divide both sides by 18 to get 1 : 4).

17. Answer C, 1/5

Explanation: You can estimate this from the pie but it is safer to calculate it by working out how many times either 35 divides into 180 or 70 divides into 360 (70 is the number of degrees of arc that the bus segment represents); both divide 5 times with a small remainder.

18. Answer A, Slightly less than twice as many people indicated that they travelled to work by bus than by car

Explanation: 35 people indicated that they travelled to work by bus while 18 indicated they travelled by car; ×2 18 = 36 which is 1 more than 35.

19. Answer B, 9

Explanation: The note to the data set states that '1 in 8 of the people who cycled to work were found to be over 65 years of age'; from this we can calculate that $72 \div 8 = 9$, the number of respondents aged over 65 who cycled to work.

20. Answer B, 48

Explanation: The note to the data states that '1 in 3 of the cyclists travelled to work by bus on rainy days', so the number of cyclists on rainy days dropped to 2/3 of 72 = $(72 \div 3 = 24 \times 2) = 48$.

Data set 3

21. Answer A, True

Explanation: The question asks if the elasticity of a balloon is greater than the elasticity of a paste and we can infer from the passage of information that this is true.

22. Answer B, False

Explanation: The question asks if the speed at which land warms is less than the speed at which water warms and it is clear from the second set of data that this is not true.

23. Answer B, False

Explanation: The question asks if, when a submarine sinks, the upward force is greater than the submarine's weight and we can tell from the last set of data that this is not true.

24. Answer B, False

Explanation: The question asks if the sea cools at a rate greater than the land and we know this to be false from the information provided in the passage.

25. Answer A, True

Explanation: The question asks if, when a submarine rises, the upward force is greater than the submarine's weight and we can judge this statement as true from the information given in the second set of data.

26. Answer C, Cannot tell

Explanation: The given information describes the relationship between the submarine's weight and its manoeuvres and not the amount of water or air in its tanks that makes those manoeuvres possible.

27. Answer A, True

Explanation: The question asks if the plasticity of a dough is less than the plasticity of a ball and it is clear from the first passage of information that this is true.

28. Answer C, Cannot tell

Explanation: The question asks if a dough has less than or equal elasticity to a paste and we cannot tell from the information provided because it would depend on the characteristics of the dough or paste.

29. Answer A, Probably true

Explanation: The question asks if at night the air temperature over the sea is greater than or equal to the temperature of the air over the land. We are told in the passage that at night the land cools faster than the sea and so the process is reversed. From this we can infer that the air over the sea is either warmer than or the same temperature as the air over the land and therefore the answer to the question is probably true.

30. Answer A, True

Explanation: The third set of data describes the principle behind the submarine's manoeuvres as upward force = submarine's weight and if the submarine remains at a given depth (does not rise or sink) then we can infer from the passage that the weight of the submarine is equal to the upward force.

Data set 4

31. Answer D, 90

Explanation: The total number of women professionals is represented by the sum of the number of women in the professions described in the pie chart entitled professional.

32. Answer A, 540

Explanation: There are 90 women employed in professional grades and 5 times as many men as this, so the total number of people employed in these grades = 90 × 5 (the number of men in professional grades) + 90 (the number of women in those grades) = 540.

33. Answer C, 1/6

Explanation: There are a total of 30 women in managerial grades and 5 of these are head of department or executive posts. The fraction therefore is 5/30 which simplifies to 1/6.

34. Answer B, 1,180

Explanation: In total (90 + 30 =) 120 women hold professional or managerial grades. Subtract this from the figure provided as a note to the data set that in total 1,300 staff are employed in these grades (1,300 – 120) to identify that 1,180 men fill these grades.

35. Answer D, > 80%

Explanation: There are 25 women in the grade of team leader out of a total of 30 women in managerial grades. This gives us the fraction of 25/30 which simplifies to 5/6, which is equal to a little over 83% (100 ÷ 6 × 5 = 83.3 recurring).

36. Answer B, 20

Explanation: There are 25 women in the grade of team manager and 5 women in head of department or executive grades combined (25 – 5 = 20).

37. Answer C, 730

Explanation: The total staff in professional and managerial grades = 1,300 and 120 women are in these grades. We have worked out the number of men in professional grades (5× the number of women in professional grades 90 × 5 =) 450. From this we can work out that 1,300 – 450 – 120 = 730 is the number of men in managerial grades.

38. Answer A, 16,250

Explanation: We are told in the notes that 8% of the total workforce at Not Yet There Corporation are employed in professional and managerial grades and can work out the size of the total workforce from this figure. 8% of the workforce = 1,300 so 1% = 1,300 ÷ 8 = 162.5, 162.5 × 100 = 16,250 or 100% of the workforce.

39. Answer D, Cannot tell

Explanation: We are able to calculate the number of men in managerial grades as a whole but do not have the information to break this figure down into the various managerial grades.

40. Answer A, 50%

Explanation: The combined total of women in Legal and Human Resources is 45 which you must express as a percentage of the total number of women in professional grades (= 90). To express 45/90 as a percentage simplify the fraction and × 100; 45/90 = ½ × 100 = 50%.

Data set 5

41. Answer A, 2,400 Nmiles

Explanation: The distance from New Zealand to Brisbane (1,200 Nmiles) can be read from the bar chart and the distance there and back is therefore 2,400 Nmiles.

42. Answer C, 2,450

Explanation: Simply total the number of passages for each month from April (300) to December (100).

43. Answer D, 1,540 miles

Explanation: In the notes we are told that an Nmile is 10% greater than a land mile so the distance from New Zealand to Tonga measured in land miles in 110% of the distance in Nmiles. 1,400 × 110% = 1,540 miles.

44. Answer B, 150,000 Nmiles

Explanation: In December there are 100 passages and 50 travel 1,000 Nmiles to Sydney, the other 50 travel 2,000 Nmiles to Fiji; this gives (50 × 1, 000 = 50,000) + (50 × 2,000 = 100,000) = 150,000 Nmiles in total.

45. Answer D, Cannot tell

Explanation: We are not given enough information regarding their relative positions and so there is insufficient information to calculate the distance between Sydney to Fiji.

46. Answer C, 1 : 5

Explanation: There are 5 stormy days and 25 non-stormy days during the period. This gives the ratio 5 : 25, which expressed in its simplest form is 1 : 5.

47. Answer A, < Half

Explanation: From a previous question the total number of passages was calculated to be 2,450. The total for the months June–September is 1,200 which is slightly less than half the total for the year.

48. Answer B, Both passages would take the same amount of time

Explanation: The passages are the same distance and both would experience adverse currents one way and favourable currents the other, so the effect of the currents is cancelled out. Therefore you would expect the passages to take the same amount of time.

49. Answer D, 294

Explanation: There were a total of 2,450 sailings. To find 12% of this total, divide by 100 to get 1% and then multiple by 12 $(2450 \div 100 = 14.5 \times 12 = 294)$.

50. Answer A, 125 hours

Explanation: The distance is 1,000 Nmiles and the speed that counts is the speed over the ground (the speed through the water will be higher because of the counter current)

The answer is therefore $1,000 \div 8 = 125$.

Data set 6

51. Answer C, Blue or indigo

Explanation: If you answered B, Yellow or green, then you brought your own (correct) knowledge to the question and failed to rely only on the information contained in the data set. In fact the wave length of the electrometric spectrum increases from gamma to microwaves but this is irrelevant to the question which states that it decreases. This means that the colour with the third-longest wave length in the visible spectrum is blue.

52. Answer C, 9 million km

Explanation: Estimate this and make the calculation more convenient by rounding up the speed of light to 300,000 km/s and multiplying it by 30 = 9 million.

53. Answer D, 1.4 mm

Explanation: The actual length of the object is irrelevant to the question. The object appears 4.2 cm long when observed through binoculars that have magnified it ×30 times so to find how long the object would appear without the binoculars divide 4.2 cm by 30 = 1.4 mm.

54. Answer B, 4,500,000 km

Explanation: Round up the speed of light in space to 300,000 km/s and deduct 1/4 or 25% (find this, for example, by dividing 300,000 by 4 = 75,000, multiply by 3 = 225,000, finally multiply by 20 to find the distance in 20 seconds = 4,500,000 km).

55. Answer A, ×5

Explanation: The most powerful single lens microscope magnifies ×375 and a microscope made from two lenses magnifies ×1,875; 375 : 1,875 = 1 : 5 or ×5 times.

56. Answer D, 28 mm

Explanation: The lowest magnification described for a single lens microscope is ×70 and 0.04 × 70 = 2.8.

57. Answer D, 3 minutes and 20 seconds

Explanation: You are told the speed of light in space = 299,972 km/s. Treat this as 300,000 and divide by 5 to find 1/5 the speed of the object = 60,000 km/s. Divide 12 million by 60,000 = 200 seconds = 3 minutes and 20 seconds.

58. Answer B, ×150

Explanation: Divide 10.125 by 0.0675 = 150.

59. Answer C, 25,000 km/s

Explanation: The speed of light through water = 299,972 ÷ 4 = 74,993 and the speed of light through glass is 1/3 of this; 74,993 ÷ 3 = 24,997.6 km/s so suggested Answer C is the best approximation.

60. Answer D, Cannot tell

Explanation: If you answered B then you assumed that the prism was made from glass and we are not told this. In the passage we are not told what a prism is made of, so we cannot determine the speed at which light might pass through it.

Data set 7

61. Answer A, $32.50

Explanation: Simply add the cost of the three optional extras to get $32.50.

62. Answer B, $675

Explanation: Each flight costs $225 and multiplied by 3 this gives the total = $675.

63. Answer A, ×3

Explanation: To find out the multiple, divide the cost of the morning flight by the cost of the afternoon flight, 225 ÷ 75 = 3, so the morning flight is 3× more expensive than the afternoon flight.

64. Answer D, $248

Explanation: Each flight costs $104 plus $20 for the luggage (=$124 per passenger) × 2 = $248.

65. Answer D, $4,482

Explanation: Multiply $63 × 54 to obtain £3,402 and add 1,080 (54 × $20) to get $4,482.

66. Answer C, $44.00

Explanation: The morning flight to destination B is $44 more than the afternoon flight. The fact that the party is a family of four with travel insurance and luggage does not affect the difference in price between these flights.

67. Answer A, $266.50

Explanation: Multiply 72 × 3 to obtain the cost of the flights and add the cost of two items of hand luggage plus the environmental offset × 3 (= 216 + 40 + 10.5) = $266.50.

68. Answer B, 30%

Explanation: The morning flight costs $80 while the afternoon flight costs $104. Take the morning flight to be 100% and find what percentage 104 represents. 100 ÷ 80 = 1.25 × 104 = 130% so the afternoon flight costs 30% more than the morning flight.

69. Answer C, $83.50

Explanation: Calculate the discount on the $75 cost of the flight by finding 80% of 75 (75 × 80 ÷ 100) = $60 then add the $20 for luggage and $3.5 for the offset to get $83.50.

70. Answer A, $174.50

Explanation: The range is the difference between the maximum and minimum values. The maximum value is the morning flight to destination A plus all further options (limited to the one item of luggage travel) = 225 + 20 + 9 + 3.50 = $257.50. The minimum cost is the morning flight to destination C with no other options but the one item of luggage = 63 + 20 = $83. The range therefore is 257.50 – 83 = $174.50.

Data set 8

71. Answer D, retail and other

Explanation: Both retail and other are predicted to increase by 15% (heavy manufacturing is predicted to decrease by 15%).

72. Answer A, –5%

Explanation: In 2005, fishing is predicted to decrease by 5% and neither to decrease nor increase in 2006.

73. Answer B, finance

Explanation: Finance in 2006 is predicted to increase by 5%. This is the lowest percentage increase predicted that year (heavy manufacturing is predicted to decrease the most and fishing the least).

74. Answer D, decrease $\geq$ 10%

Explanation: The % changes in 2006 were 5, 5, –5, –5, –5, –10 which when added together give a cumulative change of –15% or decrease $\geq$ (equal to or greater than) 10%.

75. Answer C, Other

Explanation: Other is projected to see a cumulative change of 15 in 2005 and −5 in 2006. This is a cumulative range of 20% points which is greater than, for example, retail which is projected to increase 15% in 2005 and 5% in 2006, a range of 10% points.

76. Answer B, Increase by 300,000

Explanation: Retail in 2006 is predicted to increase by 15% so you must find 15% of 2 million. 1% of 2 million is 20,000 (remove two zeros) so 15% = 20,000 × 15 = 300,000.

77. Answer A, Fishing

Explanation: Calculate the percentage fall that 37,500 represents in order to see if the sector can be identified. Do this by first adding 37,500 to 712,500 to get 750,000, which is the figure before any fall. Now calculate what 37,500 is as a percentage of 750,000. Do this by working out 1% = 7,500, then it can be seen or calculated that 5 × 7,500 = 37,500. It is then clear that 37,500 is 5% of 750,000. The sector can now be identified as fishing as it is the only one that is projected to experience a 5% decrease in 2005.

78. Answer A, 3 million

Explanation: Across the two years retail is forecast to grow by a total of 20% (15% in 2005 and 5% in 2006); the number employed in retail therefore will increase by 20% of 2,500,000 (work this out by calculating 1% first and multiplying it by 20) = 25,000 × 20 = 500,000. Add this to the 2,500,000 to get 3 million.

79. Answer D, Cannot tell

Explanation: If the number employed were equally spread across the sectors then the answer would be a 5% decrease or 1,750,000 but we do not know the proportions working in each sector so we cannot know by how many the total would change or even if the change would be positive or negative.

80. Answer C, Heavy manufacturing

Explanation: In relative terms heavy manufacturing is predicted to see the greatest improvement because it will 'improve' from a 15% decrease to a 5% decrease. Fishing will also improve from a 5% decrease to no change while retail will slip from a 15% increase to a more modest 5%.

Data set 9

81. Answer A, $2,472,000

Explanation: Find the revenue for 2007 by adding the 2006 revenue to the 2007 target. 2006 revenue = 2.4 million (this is signified by the 000,000) and 2,400,000 + 72,000 = $2,472,000.

82. Answer B, $7,400,000

Explanation: Find the total revenue for 2006 by totalling the revenue for that year.

83. Answer C, $7,546,810

Explanation: To find the total revenue in 2007, assuming targets are reached, find the total for 2006 and add it to the revenue growth for 2007. Revenue for 2006 = 7,400,000 + 134,750 revenue growth target for 2008 = $7,534,750.

84. Answer B, 2%

Explanation: You must find what 24,000 is as a percentage increase on 1,200,000; 1,200,000 = 100%, so to find the percentage increase first find 1% of 1,200,000 = 12,000 and then divide this into 24,000 = 2, a 2% increase.

85. Answer D, Hard gums

Explanation: The lowest target for 2008 is Sour cola but for 2007 it is Hard gums. On the 2007 list Sour cola and Hard gums have the lowest $ target. To establish which has the lowest target in percentage terms, calculate each target as a percentage. Sour cola = 700,000 ÷ 100 = 7,000 and 5,250 ÷ 7,000 = 0.75%, Hard gums = 1,300,000 ÷ 100 = 13,000 and 6,500 ÷ 13,000 = 0.5%. So Hard gums has the lower % target.

86. Answer C, $712,000

Explanation: In 2007 the revenue will be 705,250 (700,000 + 5250) and for 2008 it will be 1% greater. Answer C is the best estimate because 1% of 705,250 = 7,052.5 which when added to the revenue for 2007 gives a total of $712, 302.5.

87. Answer A, 2.5%

Explanation: Find the mean by totalling the percentage figures and dividing the total by 5. 3 + 1 + 4 + 2.5 + 2 = 12.5 ÷ 5 = 2.5.

88. Answer C, $2,606,500

Explanation: In 2006 Hard gums generated 1.3 million and in 2007 this figure was increased by 6,500, so the 2007 target if realized would generate 1,306,500. Combine the two figures to obtain $2,606,500.

89. Answer B, 1,850,000–1,900,000

Explanation: The revenue for 2008 will be 1.8 million + 27,000 = 1,827,000 + (2% of 1,827,000) 36,540 = 1,863,540 which falls in the range 1,850,000–1,900,000.

90. Answer D, The figures for Fruit salad in 2007 and 2008 combined give a target revenue increase of 4%

Explanation: The increase in 2007 for Fruit salad is 24,000 on 1.2 million which we previously worked out to be 2%. Add this to the percentage target for 2008 (2%) and it is clear that the statement is not valid.

Data set 10

91. Answer C, 100

Explanation: Find this total by adding the number of calls in all categories.

92. Answer A, 96

Explanation: To find the total, add together the number of calls in each range from and including the 2-minute range. 14 + 40 + 30 + 12 = 82.

93. Answer B, 54

Explanation: The number of calls with a duration of more than 1 minute but less than 4 is found by totalling the items in columns 2 and 3: 14 + 40 = 54.

94. Answer B, 0.4

Explanation: 4 conversations fell into the one-minute range so the probability of this is 4/100 which converted to a decimal = 0.4.

95. Answer D, 14 conversations lasted more than 1 minute but less than 3 minutes

Explanation: We can infer from column 2 of the diagram that 14 telephone conversations lasted longer than 1 minute but less than 3 minutes. Suggested Answer C is correct in as much as 18 conversations lasted less than 3 minutes but this is not described in column 2 but in columns 1 and 2 of the diagram.

96. Answer B, 2/5

Explanation: 40 conversations lasted 3 minutes or more but less than 4 minutes so the probability of a call lasting this long (expressed as a fraction) = 40/100 which simplifies to 2/5 (probabilities can be expressed as either fractions or decimals of 1).

97. Answer B, 140 minutes

Explanation: 40 calls fall into the 3-minute range of the diagram and these calls could last any length of time between 3 and 4 minutes (including three minutes but less than 4). Answer A has taken the length of calls to be 3 minutes (120 ÷40 = 3) each while Answer C has assumed that each call lasts 4 minutes (160 ÷ 40 = 4). Answer B is the best offered because it has taken the midpoint in the range, 3.5 minutes (40 × 3.5 = 140).

98. Answer C, Inform staff at the centre of the objectives of the survey

Explanation: Increasing the sample size of the survey, the period surveyed or ensuring that calls are selected randomly all have the potential to improve its accuracy. However, informing the staff of the objectives of the survey risks them changing their behaviour and distorting the outcome.

99. Answer A, Total duration of all calls divided by 100

Explanation: Find the mean length of the calls by dividing the sum of the length of the calls by the number of calls.

100. Answer C, 280 minutes

Explanation: To identify the best estimate, take the midpoint in each range and multiply it by the number of calls in that range to obtain (4 × .5 minutes) + (14 × 1.5 minutes) + (40 × 2.5 minutes) + (30 × 3.5 minutes) + (12 × 4.5 minutes). Then find the sum of these midpoints to obtain the best estimate = 280 minutes.

Data set 11

101. Answer A, 1960s

Explanation: The trend line for television can be seen to pass the 50% point during the 1960s.

102. Answer B, Two to three times as many

Explanation: In the 1970s the percentages using radio dropped from the low forties to the low thirties, while television remained in the low to mid-eighties. We can estimate therefore that two to three times as many households used TV rather than radio.

103. Answer D, 21 million

Explanation: You must find 70% of 30 million. Find this by multiplying $30 \times 0.7 = 21$, in this case 21 million.

104. Answer C, 1960s

Explanation: During the 1960s all three media were used in approximately 65% of households.

105. Answer C, 1950s–1980s

Explanation: Television saw a trend of incredible growth from 1950 that continued until 1980 and this could be referred to as the golden age (the best period). Suggested Answer A can be rejected because figures for television were not provided for the 1940s. Suggested Answer D can be rejected because it includes a period when television was in decline. Suggested Answer C is preferred to B because B excludes the 1950s when television experienced considerable growth.

106. Answer C, 70%

Explanation: The percentage range is the maximum minus the minimum and in the case of newspapers this is $90 - 20 = 70\%$.

107. Answer A, 1950s and 1990s

Explanation: The trend line for television does not start until the 1950s so we can reject the suggested answers that include the 1940s and it is clear from the graph that the two decades in which radio was used more than both television and newspapers were the 1950s and 1990s.

108. Answer B, 40.5 million

Explanation: We are told that 9 million = 20%, so half this, 4.5 million, = 10% and 90% = 4.5 × 9 = 40.5.

109. Answer A, Television

Explanation: Variation means change and in the period in question television saw the least change in usage.

110. Answer D, Cannot tell

Explanation: This question can only be answered if the number of households in the 1980s is known, and it is not.

Data set 12

111. Answer D, Cannot tell

Explanation: We are not given figures for 2001, 2003 and 2005 so we cannot know the total value of sales over the 6 years.

112. Answer B, 4 million

Explanation: It is clear from the graph showing the number of visitors to Venice that in 2000 there were 12 million visitors and 16 million in 2004. So the number increased by 4 million.

113. Answer B, Been consistent in all years but one

Explanation: This question is about the number of visitors who have bought Marco glass, not the ratio. It is true that the ratio of visitors who buy the glass has consistently fallen but the number has been consistent in all years but one (in 1996 it was 1 million, in all other years 2 million).

114. Answer A, ×2.5

Explanation: In 1996, 1 in 4 bought Marco glass and this compares to 1 in 10 in 2008 which is ×2.5 fewer.

115. Answer C, 12.5%

Explanation: The ratio in 2004 was 1 in 8 and to convert this to a percentage you must find 1/8 of 100 = 100 ÷ 8 = 12.5.

116. Answer D, Between $24 and $26

Explanation: In 2000 there were 12 million visitors and 1 in 6 bought some glass; sales that year were $50 million, so to find the average spend divide 12 million by 6 = 2 million and then divide 50 million by 2 million = $25.

117. Answer C, 1,440,000

Explanation: In 2000 there were 12 million visitors in total and 12% of these (12,000,000 = 100%, divide by 100 to find 1% = 120,000 × 12 = 1,440,000) were visitors from the Far East.

118. Answer B, In 2001 the value of sales in Marco glass were between $50 and $51 million

Explanation: The truth or otherwise of suggested Answer A can be read off the graph showing ratios, while the table of annual sale values cannot be used to extrapolate figures for the years not described. The open statement describes Marco glass as sold in Venice so suggested Answer C can be established as false.

119. Answer A, $2

Explanation: In a previous question we found that the average spend in 2000 was $25. In 2004 there were 16 million visitors and 1 in 8 bought Marco glass, so in 2004 sales were worth $54 million. To find the average spend in 2004, divide 16 million by 8 = 2 million (the number of visitors who bought Marco glass) and divide 54 million by 2 million = $27 which is $2 higher than the 2000 average spend.

120. Answer C, 15 million

Explanation: The graph shows that 20 million people visited Venice in 2008 and of every 4 of these 3 were women (3× as many). 20,000,000 ÷ 4 = 5,000,000 × 3 = 15,000,000 women and 5,000,000 men.

Data set 13

121. Answer C, 50

Explanation: The 30 KB point of the line on the graph passes through the figure 50 on the scale entitled cumulative frequency. This means that the size of 50 of the files is less than 30 KB.

122. Answer C, 100

Explanation: In total 300 files are included in the data and the 200 point on the cumulative frequency scale corresponds with the 90 KB point on the size scale. This means that of the 300 files included in the data, 200 are smaller than 90 KB, so 100 are 90 KB or larger.

123. Answer A, Below 75 KB

Explanation: The median is the middle item of the data and it is found at (N + 1 ÷ 2), reading across the graph at the point signified by half the sample size (in this case 300 ÷2 = 150). This point falls midway between 30 and 60 KB and so can be estimated to be 75 KB which means the median shows that 150 files are smaller than 75 KB (and 150 files are 75 KB or larger).

124. Answer D, Smaller than 120 KB

Explanation: Read across on the cumulative frequency scale at the 250 point and follow it down to the 120 KB point. This means that 250 files are smaller than 120 KB.

125. Answer B, 100

Explanation: Read up from the 60 KB point on the size of file scale to obtain 100 and from the 90 KB point to obtain 200. The difference is 100 and represents the number of files 60 KB or more but less than 90 Kb in size.

126. Answer B, 105 KB

Explanation: To find the upper quartile line, divide the number of items by 4 and then multiple by 3 = (300 ÷ 4 = 75) × 3. This gives you the point on the vertical axis at which the upper quartile would be placed = 225. Locate this point on the vertical axis and then read across the graph to the point where the line intersects it and down to the bottom axis to obtain its value = less than 105 KB (the true value for the upper quartile line would be 105 + 1).

127. Answer D, ×6

Explanation: 30 divides into 180 6 times, so a 180 KB file is 6 times bigger than a 30 KB file.

128. Answer C, 45 KB

Explanation: Find the point on the vertical axis for the lower quartile by dividing the number of items (300) by 4 = 75 and then read the point on the lower axis where this intersects with the line on the graph. Of the suggested answers, Answer C offers the best estimate.

129. Answer B, 105 KB

Explanation: There are 300 files and 75% of 300 = 0.75 × 300 = 225. Reading across the graph to the horizontal axis, this is a point between 90 and 120 KB which equals 105 KB. Note that this is also the value of the upper quartile and is also referred to as the 75th percentile.

130. Answer D, 60

Explanation: The interquartile range is the difference between the value of the upper quartile and the lower quartile. Previous questions have involved the calculation of both the upper and lower quartiles and the difference is 60.

Data set 14

131. Answer B, 6

Explanation: The graph provided data (revenue figures and forecasts) for 6 years: year 0 (actual) and years 1–5 (forecast).

132. Answer C, 120%

Explanation: This figure can be read straight off the graph.

133. Answer B, Scenario B

Explanation: To answer this question, 'picture' in your mind the figures as a curve and compare them to the 4 scenarios (otherwise calculate some of the revenues for particular years from scenarios and see which best fit the figures). The figures are quite distinctive. The rate of increase noticeably slows and the largest increase is between Yr 1 and Yr 2 ($2.5m). These characteristics should lead you to select scenario B.

134. Answer D, Scenario D

Explanation: The scenario with the least variation can be read from the graph. It is the curve that shows the least rise and fall, ranging from 105% in Yr 1 to 125% in Yr 5.

135. Answer A, 147–148%

Explanation: Extend the line and estimate the point on it for Yr 6, otherwise calculate the increase between each year (it is consistently between 7 and 8%) and add this amount to the Yr 5 percentage.

136. Answer D, 36.4m

Explanation: Calculate 140% of 26m = $26 \times 1.4 = 36.4$.

137. Answer A, More production facilities

Explanation: Only suggested Answer A related directly to the scale of output. Lowering the unit price might result in greater sales but not greater output, extending the project range would in itself not result in greater production and better distribution may improve the efficiency of the organization but would not result in an increase in production.

138. Answer C, 30m

Explanation: Find 105% of 26m and then find 110% of the new total. $26 \times 1.05 = 27.3m \times 110 = 30.03m$ rounded down to 30m.

139. Answer B, Only scenario A

Explanation: Scenario A will generate 26m × 140% in Yr 5 = 26 × 1.4 = 36.4m. The scenario with the next-highest forecast is B, which even if estimated generously amounts to 26m × 134% = 34.8m.

140. Answer A, Scenario C

Explanation: The scenario that best fits the figures can be identified as the revenue for Yr 0 is provided. Find the answer by trial. Start, for example, by calculating the figures for Yr 5 and try the most convenient first. Scenario A = 26m × 140% = 36.4m so we can rule out scenario A. Scenario C = 26m × 130m = 33.8m. This should lead you to look further at suggested Answer A to see if the other figures fit scenario C. These further investigations will lead you to conclude that suggested Answer A best fits scenario C.

Chapter 3: Twenty mini data interpretation tests

Mini test 1

1. Answer A, Monday and Wednesday

Explanation: On both Monday and Wednesday 14 vehicles are recorded as exceeding a speed limit at the four locations.

2. Answer C, 3 days

Explanation: Majority means more than half and on three days a majority of the total number of vehicles recorded as exceeding a speed limit were recorded in the 20 and 30 mph locations. The days were Monday, Wednesday and Friday.

3.   Answer C, 23

Explanation: In the introductory statement of the data set the 20 mph limit is described as a residential street and the sum of the records for this location is 20.

4.   Answer D, 68%

Explanation: On Tuesday there were a total of 23 records and 17 of these were recorded at the 50 or 70 mph locations. To answer the question find 17/23 as a percentage; do this by multiplying both the top and bottom of the fraction by 4 to give you 68/100 or 68%.

5.   Answer A, Records for Friday $\geq$ 15 and C, Records for Tuesday $\leq$ 25

Explanation: The total records for each day are Monday 14, Tuesday 23, Wednesday 14, Thursday 21 and Friday 16, which means that statements A and C are incorrect.

Mini test 2

1.   Answer A, $40

Explanation: Follow the flow diagram to the add $40 box; if you answered $65 then note that the questions asks how much is added to the order, so the answer is $40 added to the order value of $25 and not $65.

2.   Answer C, $28

Explanation: $12 is added to an order valued over $75 with a US postal address that requires express delivery, $40 is added to an order with a value over $75 with a non-US postal address that does not require express delivery and the difference is $28.

3.   Answer D, $80

Explanation: $80 is added to the non-US order while the US order qualifies for free delivery so no amount is added so the difference is $80 more.

4.   Answer B, C and D

Explanation: Follow the flow diagram along its various routes and you will see that an order under $75 for a US postal address without a promotional code is not given the option of express delivery.

5.   Answer C, Decline express delivery and D, A US postal address

Explanation: Free delivery is only an option for orders with a US postal address that do not require express delivery. Suggested Answers A and B are incorrect because orders under $75 with a promotional code may qualify and orders over $75 without a promotional code may also qualify.

Mini test 3

1.   Answer C, 5,250

Explanation: You must find 30% of 17,500. Find this by multiplying 17,500 by 0.30 = 5,250.

2.   Answer A, 14,050

Explanation: You must find the sum of 58% of 17,500 and 39% of 10,000. $17,500 \times 0.58 = 10,150$, $10,000 \times 0.39\% = 3,900$, $10,150 + 3,900 = 14,050$.

3.   Answer B, District 2

Explanation: Find which is greater of 30% of 17,500 or 57% of 10,000. $17,500 \times 0.30 = 5,250$ and $10,000 \times 0.57 = 5,700$ so the unemployed population of district 2 is the greater.

4.   Answer D, 1 : 10

Explanation: Find the sum of 12% of 17,500 and 4% of 10,000 = 2,100 + 400 =2,500, add the total populations of both districts = 27,500, minus the combined number of economically inactive = 2,500 = 25,000. You must express the ratio 2,500 : 25,000 in its simplest form; do this by cancelling the zeros and dividing both sides by 25 = 1 : 10.

5.   Answer A, 16%

Explanation: It has already been calculated that 12% of 17,500 = 2,100 and 4% of 10,000 = 400. Now find 400 as a percentage of the total economically inactive populations of both districts, 2,500. Find this by dividing 100 by 2,500 = 0.04 and multiplying it by 400 = 16 or 16%.

Mini test 4

1.   Answer C, 117

Explanation: Each young person responded to the four issues twice, once to indicate the issue that most interests them and again to indicate the issue that least interests them. Therefore the sum of responses presented in either graph identified the number of respondents.

2.   Answer A, 33

Explanation: Add the 41 responses to looking good to the 22 responses to what others think to get the sum, 63. Subtract from this the 30 who were most interested in doing well in school to get the answer 33.

3.   Answer B, Doing well in school

Explanation: In question 1 it was established that 117 young people took part in the survey and 1/3 of this = 39, and the issue that received 39 responses was Doing well in school (30 indicated it was the issue that they were most interested in and 9 indicated it was the issue they were least interested in).

4.   Answer D, 6 : 1

Explanation: 24 young people indicated that they were most interested in finding a job compared with 4 who were least interested. This gives a ratio of 24 : 4 which simplifies to 6 : 1 or 6 times as many.

5.   Answer B, 7 : 6

Explanation: 63 young people indicated that they were most interested in looking good or what others thought of them and this compares to 54 who were most interested in doing well in school or finding a job. This gives the ratio of 63 : 54 which simplifies to 7 : 6 if you divide both sides by 9.

Mini test 5

1.   Answer A, ×4

Explanation: European sales are worth 20% of the global market while the value of African sales are 5%, 20 ÷ 5 = 4 so the European market is ×4 bigger.

2.   Answer C, 8 : 1

Explanation: Find in its simplest form the ratio 56 : 7, divide both sides by 7 to get 8 : 1.

3.   Answer B, $400m

Explanation: The US share of the market is 56%; find the value of the whole market by dividing 224m by 56 = 1% of the global market = 4m and ×100 = 100% or $400m.

4.   Answer C, 3.64m

Explanation: In 2008 the global market was worth $260m and the value of the Argentinean share of the global market is 20% of 7% = first find the value of the 7% (the other share of the whole market), 260 × 7% = 18.2m × 20% (Argentina's share) = 3.64m.

5.   Answer D, 9%

Explanation: First find 20% of 260m (the value of the European market in 2008) = $52m, next find the value of the European market in 2009, $52m – $7m = $45m, now find 45m as a % of 500m (the forecast global value in 2009) 100% = 500, 1% = 5, 45 = 9%.

Mini test 6

1.   Answer C, 99

Explanation: Add 144 and 54 to get the combined total of sales and administrative applicants and find 50% of this total = 99.

2.   Answer A, 4 : 6

Explanation: Express the ratio 36 : 54 in its simplest form by dividing both sides by 9 to identify the answer as 4 : 6.

3.   Answer B, 18

Explanation: 36 professional applicants began the process of an online application and 27 (75% of 36) completed it, of these 33% passed and so 67% failed the interview, 67% of 27 = 18.

4.   Answer D, 27

Explanation: 126 applicants began the online application process and 63 (50% of 126) completed it, of these 45 (71.5% of 63) passed at the test centre and 27 (60% of 45) candidates passed the work sample stage.

5.   Answer C, 10

Explanation: Find the total of all online applicants who started the application process = 360, divide 360 by 18 = 20 and divide this by half (see the first part of the question) = 10.

Mini test 7

1.   Answer A, 38,125,000

Explanation: We are told that the board found 1/8 of the population of 305 million to be 65 or over. 305 ÷ 8 = 38.125 or 38,125,000 people aged 65 or more.

2.   Answer C, 58,560,000

Explanation: The board found that 80.8% of Americans lived in urban locations so 19.2% must live in non-urban (rural) locations. 305 million × 19.2% = 305 × 0.192 × 1 million = 58,560,000.

3.   Answer B, Greater than the UN projected rate of increase in the world population 2008–2050

Explanation: The US population is projected to increase from 305 million to 439 million, an increase of 134 million. 305 ÷ 100 = 3.05, 134 ÷ 3.05 = 43.93, clearly more than the UN projected increase for the world's population of 37%.

4.   Answer D, Cannot tell

Explanation: We are told that the trend of people moving to the most populous states will continue until a point is reached when 28% of the population are resident in those states but we are not told when this point will be reached so cannot calculate the number of Americans who will live in either Texas or California by 2050.

5.   Answer B, 274,375,000

Explanation: The US population in 2050 = 439 million, 1/4 will be under 18, 1/8 65 or over, so 5/8 of 439 million will be aged 18–64 years. 439 ÷ 8 = 54.875 × 5 274.375 × 1 million = 274,375,000.

Mini test 8

1.   Answer D, Cannot tell

Explanation: There are 270 immigrant knowledge workers at Pi Corporation but the total number of knowledge workers is not given and cannot be deduced from the information provided.

2.   Answer B, 1 : 5

Explanation: There are 54 knowledge workers from America and 270 immigrant knowledge workers in total. This gives the ratio 54 : 270 which is equivalent to 1 : 5 (54 divides into 270 exactly 5 times).

3.   Answer C: 30%

Explanation: There are 270 knowledge workers and 81 are from the continent of Africa, so express 81 as a percentage of 270, 100% = 270, 1% = 2.7, 81 ÷ by 2.7 = 30 or 30%.

4.   Answer A, 0.4

Explanation: There are 57 + 51 = 108 knowledge workers from India and Europe, so express this as a proportion of 270 (the total number of immigrant knowledge workers). 270 ÷ 108 = 2.5 and 1 ÷ 2.5 = 0.4.

5.   Answer C, 0.05

Explanation: Find 27 as a percentage of 54,000. 54,000 ÷ 27 = 2,000, 100 ÷ 2,000 = 0.05.

Mini test 9

1.   Answer B, 90,000 units

Explanation: Bangladesh = team A and production plant 2, output = 120 (labour hours) × 50 (units per hour per machine) × 15 (number of machines) = 90,000.

2.   Answer C, 6,480

Explanation: Poland is plant 1 and team B, output of Poland = 144 × 45 × 10 (number of machines), capital productivity = output ÷ no of machines; don't waste time multiplying and then dividing by the same sum (10 the number of machines), so 144 × 45 = 6,480.

3.   Answer B, 750

Explanation: Labour productivity = output ÷ labour hours, so 120 × 50 × 15 = 90,000 ÷ 120. = 750; don't waste time multiplying and then dividing by 120 – simply multiply 50 × 15 = 750.

4.   Answer A, 80%

Explanation: Capital utilization = output as a percentage of maximum output. There are 10 machines in the plant in Poland and each is capable of a maximum output of 8,100 so maximum output = 81,000, actual output = 64,800 (144 × 45 × 10); find 64800 as a percentage of 81,000. Divide top and bottom by 810 to get 80/100 or 80%.

5.   Answer D, 70,000

Explanation: 2,760 (Mexico's capital productivity) = output ÷ 20 (the number of machines at the Mexico plant) so the output of Mexico is 2,760 × 20 = 55,200. In previous answers the output of Poland was established as 64,800 and Bangladesh 90,000; the mean is found by dividing the sum of these by 3 = 55,200 + 64,80 + 90,000 = 210,000 ÷ 3 = 70,000.

Mini test 10

1.   Answer C, 1937
Explanation: 2017 – 80 =1937.

2.   Answer A, 24

Explanation: In 1990 the population of Cuba is stated as 12.5m and the United States as 300m. You must establish which of the suggested answers is the equivalent to 300m: 12.5m, divide 300 by 12.5 = 24, so for every Cuban there are 24 Americans.

3.   Answer D, 250

Explanation: Subtract the estimate number of couples in 2010 from the total for 1990, 2250 + 2500 + 1000 = 5750, 3000 + 2000 + 1000 = 6000 so it is estimated that 250 fewer couples will celebrate in 2010 than 1990.

4.   Answer C, 1 in 50,000

Explanation: In 1990 there were 3,000 couples in the United States who has celebrated their 80th wedding anniversary from a population of 300m. A couple comprises two people so find the equivalent to 6,000/300m. Cancelling the zeros gives you 6/300,000 = 1 in 50,000.

5.   Answer D, Mexico between 1990 and 2000

Explanation: The question refers to when the population DID grow by the greatest percentage, so ignore all the estimates. This leaves just three percentage increase calculations to undertake. 300m–312m: 300 = 100%, 3 = 1%, 12 = 4% (United States); 100m–105m = 5% (Mexico); 12.5m–13m: 12.5 = 100%, 0.125 = 1% 0.5 = 4% (Cuba). It is clear therefore that Mexico saw the greatest increase in population in the period at 5%.

Mini test 11

1.   Answer D, 2,160,000

Explanation: The previous total number of jobs in the South West was 2,300,000 minus from this 140,000 to find the new total = 2,160,000.

2.   Answer A, –495,000

Explanation: Total all job gains and minus all job losses (33,000 + 70,000 + 172,000 =) 275,000 – (360,000 + 270,000 + 140,000=) 770,000 = –495,000.

3.   Answer A, South

Explanation: Express the change in each of the regions as a fraction of the previous total for that region. The region with the second-largest relative variation will correspond to the second-greatest fraction. South = 360,000/2,400,000 = 36/240, South East = 270,000/1,600,000 = 27/160 and South West = 140,000/2,300,000 = 14/230. Reject the South West as the smallest, then investigate if the South or South East is the largest. You should be able to see at a glance that the South East 27/160 is larger than 36/240 and so the South East has the largest variation and so South the second largest.

4.   Answer A, South

Explanation: The South has the most jobs under the previous totals but suffered the most job losses, which resulted in the South falling to the region with the third-highest number of jobs (new first North West, second South West).

5.   Answer C, 1,833,000

Explanation: The total increase in jobs was 275,000. 12% of this total = 33,000 and the region that experienced this increase in jobs is the North. The new total for jobs in this region is 1,800,000 + 33,000 = 1,833,000.

Mini test 12

1.   Answer A, 3,375

Explanation: Total the number of Bottlenosed, Striped, Risso's Atlantic, Striped and Common dolphins to get the total 3,375 sightings.

2.   Answer A, 1 : 3

Explanation: There were 3,375 sightings of dolphins and 1,125 whales. This gives a total of 4,500 sightings and a ratio of 1,125 : 3375 which cancels to 1 : 3.

3.   Answer D, 7%

Explanation: There were 4,500 sightings in total and of these 315 were of sperm whales, so find 315 as a percentage of 4,500. 4,500 ÷ 100 = 45, so 1% = 45, 315 ÷ 45 = 7 or 7%.

4.   Answer C, 1 : 3 : 2

Explanation: There were respectively 310, 930, 620 sightings of Bottlenosed, Striped and Risso's dolphins and you need to find which of the suggested answers is the equivalent to this. Divide all three by 310 to establish that the number of sightings is equal to the ratio 1 : 3 : 2.

5.   Answer B, 72°

Explanation: The pie chart = 360° and Common dolphins were sighted a total of 900 times out of the total of 4,500 sightings. Find the angle with $900/4500 \times 360 = 1/5 \times 360 = 72$ or 72°.

Mini test 13

1.   Answer A, 6

Explanation: From the example of the Punjab it can be established that APS is calculated by dividing average savings by average income and then using this information to calculate the APS for population 1, $1,400/8,400 = 6$.

2.   Answer A, 2

Explanation: The population with the highest value APS can be taken to be the population that places the least emphasis on the need to save. Look to the suggested answers to realize that you need only decide between populations 2, 3 and 6. Rule out population 3 by roughly estimating the APS. Calculate the APS for populations 2 and 6 to establish that they are 12 and 11 respectively. Population 2 therefore has the highest APS and places the least emphasis on the need to save.

3.   Answer B, 6.2

Explanation: The APS for population 5 is given while the APS for populations 1 and 2 were calculated in the previous questions; to find the APS for the three populations total the three individual APS and divide by 3. 6 + 12 + 0.7 = 18.7 ÷ 3 = 6.2

4.   Answer B, 5

Explanation: The new level of savings for population 6 would become $1,700 + $2,040 = $3,740; find the new APS by dividing $18,700 by $3,740 = 4.

5.   Answer D, $1,987.5

Explanation: Average income has increased by $7,950 (from $31,800 to $39,750). This = 1/4 or 125%. For APS to remain the same, saving must increase by the same proportion or percentage. 7,950 ÷ 4 = $1,987.5

Mini test 14

1.   Answer D, $199.50

Explanation: In 2004 the price of a ream increased by 5% but the purchaser received a 5% discount on a bulk purchase of 100 reams. $2 × 105% = $2.10, $2.10 × 95% = 1.995, so each ream would cost $1.995, but the question asked how much would a customer pay for 100 reams so multiply this by 100 to give you $199.50.

2.   Answer A, 400,000

Explanation: In 2008 Just Paper sold 93.9 × 1000 tons and in 2009 94.3 × 1000 tons = [2009] 94,300 – [2008] 93,900 = 400 tons more in 2009. You are told that a ton = 1,000 reams so in 2009 Just Paper sold 400 × 1,000 = 400,000 more reams than in 2008.

3.   Answer C, 6%

Explanation: Over the period shown the mean rate was 5 + 11 + 7.5 + 12.5 = 36%; find the annual mean rate by dividing by the number of years over the period shown but note that period is 2004 to 2010 = 6 years, 36 ÷ 6 = 6 or 6%.

4.   Answer B, $167.7m

Explanation: A straight line trend between 5% in 2004 and 11% in 2006 gives 8% for 2005 (5 + 11 = 16 ÷ 2 = 8). In 2003 a ream was priced at $2 and $2 + 5% in 2004 = $2.10, so $2.10 × 108% in 2005 = $2.26. In 2005 Just Paper sold 74.2 × 1000 tons of Universal White, before any discounts, therefore total sales were worth 74.2 × 1,000 × 1,000 (the number of reams in each ton) = 74.2m × 2.26 = 167.692m and the closest estimate is B, $167.7m.

5.   Answer C, 11.5%

Explanation: If you are short of time then you could extend the line visually, otherwise find the mean increase across the four entries and add to this the common difference between the entries. The mean increase across the four entries is (36% ÷ 4 =) 9%, the differences are (5% to 11% =) +6%, (11% to 7.5% =) –3.5%, (7.5% to 12.5% =) +5% giving a common difference of (11 – 3.5 = 7.5 ÷3 =) +2.5%. Based on this an estimate for 2012 = 9 + 2.5 = 11.5%.

Mini test 15

1.   Answer B, 70 days

Explanation: It is clear from the flow diagram that the final warning is issued when the invoice is 60 days old and the case referred to the solicitor after a further 10 days.

2.   Answer A, 45

Explanation: 30 days ago, 145 invoices were referred to the solicitor and from the flow diagram it can be established that there are four possible outcomes: the invoice can be disputed or the liability denied (91 fit these categories), or the liability can be admitted (9 invoices fall into this category); this leaves 45 which must belong to the remaining category.

3.   Answer C, $315.5

Explanation: You do not have time to calculate fully the average value but by selecting the most convenient figures and undertaking the calculation in these cases you should then feel confident in selecting suggested Answer C as the correct answer.

4.   Answer D 80%

Explanation: 30 days ago, $1.26m was tied up pending court cases and you must find which of the suggested answers best represents 1m as a percentage of this. 1.26m = 100%, 10% = 0.126, 1 ÷ 0.126 = 7.93, so the best estimate is 80%.

5.   Answer B, 63%

Explanation: Find 50 as a percentage of 79; approximate as 50/80 = 5/8, multiply both by 12.5 = 62.5% or suggested Answer B, 63%.

Mini test 16

1.   Answer C, 3

Explanation: To find the number of births first divide the population by 1,000 and then multiply by the rate of births per 1,000. In country 3, 58,000,000 ÷ 1,000 = 58,000 × 2.4 = 139,200 births.

2.   Answer A, 1

Explanation: Find the population density by dividing the population by the km² occupied by the country. In the case of country 1, 7,800,000 ÷ 77,474 = approx 100.67 and is by far the closest to 100 people per km².

3.   Answer C, ×15

Explanation: Country 2 occupies an area of 450,000km² and country 3 an area of 30,000km². Cancel these down to 450 and 30 and divide 450 by 30 to get ×15.

4.   Answer D, 1/126

Explanation: The world population = 150m × 63 (the number of people per km²) = 9,450 m, the population of the three countries = 75m so find 75/9450 as an equivalent fraction to one of the suggested answers. 9450 ÷ 75 = 126 or 1/126 of the world population.

5.   Answer A, 1

Explanation: The population of country 2 is decreasing (the death rate per 1,000 is higher than the birth rate) so the correct answer is either country 1 or country 3. The population of country 1 is increasing by (15.3 – 9.9) = 5.4 per 1,000, country 3 is increasing by 0.7 per 1,000. Multiply by size of country to find rate in real terms. Country 1 = 7,800,000 ÷ 1000 = 7800 × 5.4 = 42,120, country 2 = 58,000,000 ÷ 1,000 = 58,000 × 0.7 = 40,600, so country 1 population is increasing the most in real terms.

Mini test 17

1.   Answer C, 266

Explanation: The neighbourhood has a population of 1749, 1 in 3 are aged 18–59 = 588 and 900 are aged 60 or more. This leaves 266 aged 0–17 years.

2.　Answer C, 63,750

Explanation: 7/8 of the 50,000 aged 18–59 will not vote = 43,750 + 4/5 of the 25,000 of the 60 or 60+ cohort = 63,750.

3.　Answer B, 479

Explanation: 37% of 18–59-year-olds are positive 588 × 37% = 217.56 rounded up to 218, + 29% of the 60 and over cohort = 900 × 29% – 261 gives total 479.

4.　Answer A, 634

Explanation: There are 25,000 people in the city aged 60 or more and 900 in your neighbourhood = 24,100 outside your neighbourhood; there are also 25,000 people aged 0–17 living in the city and 266 of these live in your neighbourhood = 24,734 not in your neighbourhood. 24,734 – 24,100 = 634.

5.　Answer B, Your neighbourhood makes up less than 2% of the population of the city overall

Explanation: Suggested Answer A is incorrect because the same number of people in the city overall are aged 60 or more and between the age of 0–17, C is incorrect because 1,488 people in your neighbourhood are old enough to vote (18 or older). D is incorrect because 180 people aged 60 or more plan to vote compared with 65 people in the 18–59 cohort. Suggested Answer B is true, the city population is 100,000 and the neighbourhood 1,749 which as a percentage of the population overall is 1.749 so less than 2%.

Mini test 18

1.　Answer C, $1,711,140

Explanation: The value reduces by 5% per annum so in yr 2 it is worth 95% of 1,896,000 = 1,801,200 and in yr 3 = 1,711,140.

2.   Answer A, $161,200

Explanation: First year revenue for 100035 and 100041 = 94,800 + 66,400 = 161,200.

3.   Answer C, 2

Explanation: They will lose money on products 100036 and 100037. All unit values will decrease by 5%; in the case of 100036 and 100037 they will drop just below the cost price to 0.2565 (cost price 0.26)and 0.7885 (cost price 0.79) respectively.

4.   Answer D, 100038

Explanation: Discount products 100036 and 100037 because you have already established their margins as the lowest. Calculate the margins for year 1 (the product will remain the relative best for all years); the margin on $100038 = 0.35 - 0.28 = 0.07$, $0.28 \div 0.07 = 4$, $100 \div 4 = 25\%$ ($0.35 = 125\%$ of 0.28). The next best margin on a key product is $100040 = 0.25 - 0.21 = 0.04$, $0.21 \div 0.04 = 5.25$, $100 \div 5.25 = $ approx 19%.

5.   Answer B, 3

Explanation: You don't have time to calculate the new values for all 8 products so eliminate the most expensive as obviously too expensive. Next, estimate the 'most expensive' that if inflated by 280% will remain below $1. Undertake that calculation and be sure to note how many other 'cheaper' products will also qualify. For example, calculated for product $100038 = 0.35 \times 280\% = 0.35 \times 2.8 = 0.98$ (under $1), this means that products 100036 and 100040 will also qualify. So the answer is that 3 of Shinning's products can be marked up by 280% and be sold at $1 or less.

Mini test 19

1.   Answer A, 248

Explanation: 80 crimes are reported in the first bar chart while 168 are detailed in the second (young people's first and most recent) = 248.

2.   Answer C, 9

Explanation: 25 identified buy alcohol as the reason for their first crime, 28 for their most recent crime = 3, 30 identified buy drugs as the reason for their first crime, 36 for their most recent = 6, giving the total of 9.

3.   Answer A, 3/10

Explanation: 20 + 4 = 24 out of 80. Divide both top and bottom by 8 = 3/10.

4.   Answer D, 62.5%

Explanation: Add all crimes involving misuse or purchase of drugs or alcohol = 155. Estimate this as a percentage of all crimes = 248. Speed up this calculation by rounding up 248 to 250 (remembering that this will slightly understate the answer). 100 ÷ 250 = 0.4, 155 × 0.4 = 62, look to the suggested answers and select 62.5% as the answer that allows for the fact that your rounding of 248 to 250 is a slight underestimation.

5.   Answer D, 30%

Explanation: 80 = 100%, 100 ÷ 80 = 1.25, 12 × 1.25 = 15 and 36 × 1.25 = 45, which means that 30% more of the cohort gave as the reason drug or alcohol misuse over trouble at home.

Mini test 20

1. Answer B, 4%

Explanation: It is stated in the data set that in 2003 each outlet was located in a residential area with an average population of 135,000 and that each outlet has 5,400 customers a day. The answer to the question therefore is found by expressing 5,400 as a percentage of 135,000. Find this by first establishing 1% of 135,000 = 1,350 and then divide 5,400 by 1,350 = 4%.

2. Answer A, An across-the-board cut of 2.5% in the price of all products

Explanation: A price reduction of 2.5% would still leave Mare's prices at almost 10% above those typically charged by the competitor and so do very little if anything to assist Mare's management team in meeting the threat. Offering a series of 'added value' services not offered by the competitor, such as free home delivery, longer store opening hours and online shopping, would improve the customers' perception of Mare in terms of the value for money offered (Mare's customers quoted value for money as the most important factor in deciding where they shop).

3. Answer D, $940,000

Explanation: Find the amount of profit on each of the years and the answer to the question is the difference between them. The value of sales in 2003 was $29.5m and in 2008 $34.2m and over the period Mare has shown an average 20% profit margin on the value of these sales. 29.5m × 20 % = 29.5m × 0.2 = 5.9m, 34.2 × 0.2 = 6.84. The difference is 0.94m or $940,000.

4.   Answer B and C

Explanation: Maintaining a small premium in prices over the competitor (suggested Answer A) will still involve a cut in prices and so still risks the impression that quality has been cut too. Only cutting the price of items that the competitor does not sell will still leave those items open to the conclusion that quality has been cut. Both suggested Answers B and C provide the customer with some form of assurance that quality is unaffected by a price cut.

5.   Answer C, 2.394m

Explanation: The forecast was 10% less than 2008 = 34.2m × 90% = 34.2 × 0.9 = 30.78m, the actual for 2009 was 3% below 2008 = 34.2 × 97% = 33.174. The difference is 2.394m.

Chapter 4

Test 1

Data set 1

1.   Answer A, $2,400,000

Explanation: It is stated in the introductory text that the fixed costs for the calculations are $3m and that total costs are derived by adding fixed and variable costs. Therefore find the variable costs by subtracting the fixed costs from the total costs in scenario B.

2.   Answer C, 250,000

Explanation: Divide 4,500,000 by 18 to get 250,000.

3.   Answer B, 132,349

Explanation: The number of units in scenario A was calculated to be 250,000. You could find the number in scenario C by dividing 6,477,000 by 16.94 but without a calculator this may take too long so instead look to the suggested answers and adjust the calculation to make it more convenient. The obvious thing to do is round 16.94 up to 17 and divide 6,477,000 by 17 = 381,000 (if you cannot do this calculation without a calculator then you may well need to revise your command of the multiplication tables and/or improve your mental arithmetic). 381,000 − 250,000 = 131,000. Note you rounded up so the correct answer will be a bit higher; this should lead you to ignore suggested Answer A and select B as correct.

4.   Answer C, 120%

Explanation: The total cost increased from $4,500,000 to $5,400,000. You can ignore the zeros to make the sum more convenient, and find the percentage increase on 45 to give 54. 100% = 45, 10% = 4.5, so 110% = 49.5 and 120% = 154.

5.   Answer D, New unit cost × 97% = $18

Explanation: If variable costs are $750,000 then total costs (variable plus fixed) will be $3,750,000. This total cost is consistent with the change between the total costs in scenarios A and B (identified in Q4) 3,750,000 × 120% = 4,500,000. It is reasonable therefore to expect the new unit cost to follow the trend in unit costs in Scenarios A and B. Take $18 = 100%, 1% = 0.18, 18 − 17.46 = 0.54, 0.54 ÷ 0.18 = 3, so there is a 3% reduction between the unit price of $18 and $17.46, namely new unit cost × 103% = $18. Note, $18 × 103% does not equal the new unit price any more than $17.46 × 103% = $18 (investigate this with a calculator if it is not obvious).

Data set 2

6.   Answer C, 2%

Explanation: The rate in Australia was cut at the end of 2007 from 5% to 4.5%; the rate in Canada remained at 6.5%, a difference of 2%.

7.   Answer B, 40%

Explanation: Australian exports of wheat in 2006 were worth $41.677 million, and you are told the increase is $16.5778 million. Speed up this calculation by rounding the figures to more convenient sums. For example, find 16 as a percentage of 41, 16 ÷ 0.41 = a little over 39. Then look to the suggested answers: reject A because the amount by which you rounded the sums would not increase the percentage this much, reject C and D because you rounded the sums down and this would mean that the actual percentage would be higher.

8.   Answer D, At the end of 2008 Australia's rate was 3% above the inflation rate while Canada's was 1.5% below inflation

Explanation: At the end of 2008 it was Canada's rate that was 3% above inflation and Australia's rate that was 1.5% below inflation and not the other way around as stated in the suggested answer.

9.   Answer B, 1/3 more than the worth of its coal exports

Explanation: Coal exports were worth $354m and timber $472m, divide 354 by 3 = 118, add (the original sum) 354 = 472 (the value of timber exports that year).

10. Answer A, 10%

Explanation: Combined exports (iron ore and coal) in 2006 were worth $774.768m while combined exports in 2007 were worth $852.2448. Estimate the answer by calculating 775 × 110% = 775 +77.5 = 852.5, close enough for you to know that suggested Answer A is correct.

Data set 3

11. Answer A, 1/4

Explanation: You are told that 111m out of 148m live in urban locations so 37/148 live in rural locations. 148 ÷ 37 = 4 so 1/4 live in rural locations.

12. Answer D, Between 1990 and 2010

Explanation: The graph showing urban population trends shows that the urban populations in Africa and Europe were the same in 1990 and that Africa had overtaken Europe by 2010, therefore the size of Africa's urban population overtook that of Europe between 1990 and 2010.

13. Answer B, 54%

Explanation: The table shows that 62% of sample 2 failed to achieve level 3 and the note states that the female rate is 16% behind that of men. To find the female rate we first need the male rate for 2010 (this is not 62%) in the graph entitled rate of literacy (level 3) by gender. The male rate in 2010 is given as 70%. 70 – 16 = 54% for the female rate.

14. Answer C, 1 : 5

Explanation: There were 46 million Europeans and 229 million Asian participants, so find the estimate closest to 46 : 229. Round the sum to 46 : 230 (230 divided by 46 = 5); best estimate therefore is 1 : 5.

15. Answer A, 23.46 million

Explanation: 49% of sample 2 failed to reach level 3 so 51% succeeded. Find 51% of sample size: 46 million = 46 × 0.51 = 23.46 or 23.46 million.

16. Answer C, ×3

Explanation: In 1970 the three continents' urban population = 0.1 + 0.7 + 0.3 = 1.1 billion. In 2010 the urban population has grown to 0.8 + 1.9 + 0.6 = 3.3 billion, which is ×3 greater than the 1970 total.

17. Answer A, 8

Explanation: You are told that the gap in 2010 is 16 percentage points. The gap in 1970 is found on the graph rate of literacy by gender, which shows the male rate at 45% and the female rate at 21%, a gap of 24 percentage points. The gap between 1970 and 2010 has closed 8 percentage points: 24 − 16 = 8.

18. Answer A, Just over 50 million

Explanation: It was previously established that 54% of women failed to reach level 3, so 46 reached that level. The size of sample 2 is 229 million, half of which is women. 229 ÷ 2 = 114.5m × 46% = 114.5 × 0.46 = 52.67 million or suggested Answer A, just over 50 million.

19. Answer B, 320 million

Explanation: The urban populations graph shows that in 1990, 0.5 billion Africans were urban and the graph of the rate of literacy shows that 64% of urban Africans were literate to level 3. Find 64% of 500 million, 500 × 0.64 = 320 million.

20. Answer C, Women from sample 1

Explanation: population A = 46m × 51% = 23.46, B = 229m × 38% = 87.02m, C = 229m × 50% = 114.5m, D = 111m (see note).

21. Answer D, Cannot tell

Explanation: The figures for 2003 and 2005 are not provided so a total for the period cannot be established.

22. Answer B, $117,000

Explanation: The value of sales for market A in 2006 was 115 and 119 in 2008. Find the mean by adding these two values and dividing by 2. 234 ÷ 2 = 117

23. Answer B, ×6.25

Explanation: Sales figures for market A total $475,000 while those for market B total $76,000 and 76,000 divides 6.25 times into 475,000.

24. Answer A, Lower the price

Explanation: One of the market research findings regarding market B is that customers perceive higher price to imply higher quality and for this reason we can infer that by lowering the price we risk undermining the customer perception of quality and this would not help sales.

25. Answer C, 20,700

Explanation: Sales in 2006 were 18,000 and the figures for 2007 were 115% better; 18,000 × 115 = 20,700.

26. Answer C, Competitor brands are winning Royal Tea's market share

Explanation: The sales of Royal Tea in market A have remained relatively consistent (but for the exception of 2006) and so do not support the finding that competitor brands are winning Royal Tea's market.

27. Answer A, $102,000

Explanation: The ratio of the value of sales in 2002 was 120 : 20, which reduces to 6 : 1. If we divide 119 by the same ratio we get 102 : 17 (divide 119 by 7 = 17 × 6 = 102).

28. Answer B, $7,000

Explanation: Sales in markets A and B combined in 2004 were 121,000 + 19,000 = $140,000, sales in 2006 in both markets were $115,000 + $18,000 = $133,000. $140,000 – $133,000 = $7,000.

29. Answer A, $2,800,000

Explanation: 140,000 = 5%. To find 100% divide 140,000 by 5 = 28,000 and multiply by 100 = 2,800,000.

30. Answer C, $3000

Explanation: Find 0.57 as a percentage of $3.80 and multiply $20,000 by that percentage. 3.80 = 100%, 1% = 3.80 ÷ 100 = 0.038, 0.57 ÷ 0.038 = 15, so the profit = 15%; 20,000 (the value of sales that year) × 15% = $3,000

Test 2

Data set 1

1.   Answer C, 5.156 billion

Explanation: Add the 7 entries plus the 1.7 billion second language speakers. If you look to the suggested answers as you undertake the calculation then you will find the correct answer after completing only the second column as Answer C is the only one that ends with 56.

2.   Answer B, 1/7th

Explanation: 5.156 – 1.700 = 3,456, the number who speak the 7 languages (as first language). Total Spanish and French speakers = 500 million. Now find nearest equivalent fraction to 500/3,456 = 1/7.

3.   Answer D, Cannot tell

Explanation: We can establish how many languages are predicted to die out but not how many people currently speak them, nor can we infer or deduce this number from the information given.

4.   Answer D, 2,755

Explanation: Find 72.5% of 3,800 = 3,800 × 0.725 = 2,755.

5.   Answer A, 1 in 12

Explanation: 2/7 of the world's population = 3.456 billion (the number of first-language speakers of the 7 languages), the world total population then = 3.456 ÷ 2 × 7 = 12.096 billion. There are 1 billion first-language speakers of Chinese, therefore 1 in 12 is the closest estimate.

Data set 2

6.   Answer C, 10,000

Explanation: The figures for each fishery can be read directly from the tables. The difference is 10,000 tonnes.

7.   Answer B, 19,500

Explanation: The quota started in 1995 at 30,000 tonnes and decreased by 1,500 tonnes a year after 7 years (2002). The quota was 10,500 tonnes lower at 19,500 tonnes.

8.   Answer A, Tonnes sold were the same as quotas

Explanation: First calculate the quota for 2000 = 30,000 – 5 × 1,500 = 7,500 = 22,500 tonnes. Tonnes sold that year = 17,500 tonnes Atlantic tuna plus 5,000 tonnes Mediterranean = 22,500 tonnes. So tonnes sold were the same as quotas.

9.   Answer C, 2015

Explanation: 30,000 ÷ 1,500 = 20 years, 1995 + 20 = 2015.

10. Answer B, 2,500 tonnes

Explanation: The quota for 2010 = 7,500 tonnes (2010 – 1995 = 15 × 1,500 = 22,500, 30,000 – 22,500 = 7,500). The quote for 2011 = 1/2 2010 = 7,500 ÷ 2 = 3,750 tonnes. 3,750 ÷ 3 = 1,250 tonnes, Atlantic share = 1,250 × 2 = 2,500 tonnes.

Data set 3
11. Answer B, 17%

Explanation: Over the 5 years December hourly wages increased from \$13 to \$15.21, an increase of \$2.21. Find the percentage increase by dividing 2.21 by 13 and multiply the result by 100, 2.21 ÷ 13 = 0.17 × 100 = 17%. The December wage therefore increased by 17% over the 5 years. D is wrong because the increase was \$2.21, not \$15.21.

12. Answer C, \$590.40

Explanation: Production workers earned \$14.4 an hour and worked an average of 41 hours, 14.4 × 41 = 590.40.

13. Answer D, 8%

Explanation: The retail assistant average working week decreased from 47.5 to 43.7 hours, a decrease of 3.8 hours. Find the percentage decrease, divide 3.8 by 47.5 and multiply by 100, 3.8 ÷ 47.5 = 0.08 × 100 = 8%.

14. Answer C, $9.00

Explanation: Find the annual average rate by totalling the monthly averages and dividing by 12. Speed this up by subtotalling the monthly figures that are the same. ($8 × 9 months) $72 + (11.5 × 2) 23 + 13 = 108 ÷ 12 = 9.

15. Answer A, $74

Explanation: June 2002 = $15.5 an hour × 40 hours a week = $620, Aug 2000 = $14 an hour × 39 hours = $546; 620 – 546 = 74.

Data set 4

16. Answer B, 2010 will match 2006 in terms of the level of street crime recorded

Explanation: You can project the line visually to project that crimes will reach a total of 4,400 in 2010.

17. Answer D, 4,200

Explanation: The graph shows the total recorded street crimes broken down into those involving violence and vehicles, and others. Therefore the total number of recorded crimes is simply read off the (000s) axis. 11,180 is obtained if you incorrectly add the three figures displayed in the bar chart.

18. Answer C, 3,500

Explanation: Street crimes that did not involve vehicles = other street crimes + street crimes that involved violence. In 2007, 3,300 other street crimes were reported and (3,800 – 3,600) 200 street crimes involved violence = 3,500.

19. Answer B, Fewer crimes involving vehicles were recorded in 2009 than in 2008

Explanation: In 2008, 3,900 – 3,740 = 160 crimes involving vehicles were recorded; in 2009, 3,560 – 3,420 = 140 crimes involving vehicles were recorded. So B, Fewer crimes involving vehicles were recorded in 2009 than in 2008 is true.

20. Answer D, 20%

Explanation: In 2006, 4,040 – 3160 = 880 crimes involved vehicles, all recorded street crimes that year = 4,400, 880 as a percentage of 4,400 = 880 ÷ 44 = 20%.

Data set 5

21. Answer A, $1,750

Explanation: The total for the list, of course, is $1,750.

22. Answer D, 1,200

Explanation: It is possible that every member of staff in a sales position could choose to attend the pubic-speaking course, in which case the number of delegates would be 60% of the total of 2,000 = 1,200.

23. Answer B, 3%

Explanation: We are told that the total wage bill is $42 million and the personal development budget is $1,260,000. Calculate 1% of the budget to get (42,000,000 ÷ 100 =) 420,000, and then you can readily see that the budget = 3%.

24. Answer C, $21,000

Explanation: We are told that the wage bill is 42,000,000 and that there are 2,000 staff. To find the average we divide the wage bill by the number of staff. 42,000,000 ÷ 2,000 = 21,000.

25. Answer A, $1,050

Explanation: We are told that staff can spend to a maximum of 5% of the average salary on personal development courses. To find the figure we need to find 5% of 21,000 (the average salary). $21,000 \div 100 = 210$, $210 \times 5 = 1050$.

26. Answer C, $162,000

Explanation: We are told that 60% of staff are in sales positions, so calculate $2,000 \times 60\% = 1,200$, find 90% of this subtotal, $1,200 \times 90\% = 1080$, and multiply this by the cost per course, $150, = 162,000.

27. Answer B, 2

Explanation: Each member of staff can spend to a maximum of 1,050 on courses but an employee who is neither a manager nor in a sales position is restricted to 3 courses, 2 of which cost $475 each. This means that they can attend only 2 of the 3 courses before they exceed their personal budget.

28. Answer D, 220

Explanation: We are told that Q.com employ 2,000 staff and 89% are based in the United States. This means that 11% are not based in the United States and 11% of $2,000 = 2,000 \times 0.11 = 220$.

29. Answer D, 4

Explanation: Sales staff can choose from a total of 5 courses, 3 of which cost $150 each and two cost $475 each. From this we can deduce that the maximum number of courses someone in a sales position can attend is 4 (3 at $150 and 1 at $475).

30. Answer A, $975

Explanation: The budget is $1,050 (5% of the average wage) and the maximum of this that a manager can spend is $975. This can be arrived at, for example, if the manager attends the demonstrating leadership course ($350), 1 of the courses priced at $475 and 1 priced at $150.

Test 3

Data set 1

1.   Answer A, 9,635,000

Explanation: The number of dollar millionaires a year ago = 94% of this year's figure. 10,250,000 × 94% (10,250,000 ÷ 100 = 102,500 × 94) = 9,635,000.

2.   Answer C, 1/24

Explanation: There are 10,250,000 dollar millionaires and 427,000 of these are from China. Find the equivalent fraction of 427,000/10,250,000 = 427/10,250; divide top and bottom by 427 to get nearest estimate 1/24 (note 427 × 24 = 10,248).

3.   Answer E, Nepal

Explanation: A billion = 1,000 million (this is the most widely accepted definition); the country's yearly income is found by multiplying the per capita income by the population and 28 × 179 = 5012, so 28m × 179 = 5.012 billion.

4.   Answer D, Mozambique has the second-lowest yearly income.

Explanation: The lowest yearly income is Somalia, then Mozambique. We cannot establish C as true because individual Chinese dollar millionaires may have more than a million dollars each. No information is provided as to the number of millionaires in Ethiopia and the figure cannot be deduced from the information given. We are not told of France's position in the league (only that China has surpassed it) and cannot deduce from the information provided that it is now in 6th position because it is possible that other countries also surpassed France.

5.   Answer B, $900,000

Explanation: There are 400,000 French dollar millionaires so divide 36 billion by 400,000. 36 billion = 36,000,000,000; cancel the zeros to get $360,000 \div 4 = 900,000$.

Data set 2

6.   Answer B, $1.2

Explanation: The previous spend was $20 and has increased by 6%. The increase equals 6% of $20 = 20 \div 100 = 0.2 \times 6 = 1.2$, or $1.2.

7.   Answer B, $104,940

Explanation: The average number of customers in January was $550 \times$ the 9 stores = 4,950 customers $\times$ the new average spend = $4,950 \times 21.2 = 104,940$.

8.   Answer B, $763.2

Explanation: There are 9 restaurants and each week they will refund 4 meals at an average price of £20 $\times$ 106%; $20 \times 106\% = \$21.20$; $4 \times 9 \times 21.2 = \$763.2$.

9.   Answer A, 0.00551

Explanation: The total number of meals was 2,900 ÷ 16 = 181.25 per average week, of which 4 are returned. Probability = 1 ÷ 181.25 = 0.00551, but you do not have time for this second calculation and your familiarity with numbers should lead you to reject suggested Answer B, 0.005, as the probability of 1 in 200 given indicates that only suggested Answer A is greater than this so it must be correct.

10. Answer C, Close to 40,000

Explanation: We are told that there are 9 restaurants in the chain and the average number of diners over the period shown = 2,900 = 68% of capacity. 1% = 2,900 ÷ 68 = approximately 43; 100% = 4300 × 9 = 38,700 or close to 40,000.

Data set 3

11. Answer D, 1.16%

Explanation: Over the 7 years shown there are 1,160 deaths predicted. To express this as a percentage of the original 100,000, move the decimal place 3 places = 1.16.

12. Answer A, 1974

Explanation: Subtract 35 from 2009 = 1974.

13. Answer B, 284

Explanation: Find the number of deaths by 35 = 100,000 − 96,454 = 3,546, now find 8.% of 3,546 = 283.68 or 284 deaths.

14. Answer C, 145

Explanation: There are predicted to be 1,160 deaths between the ages of 35 and 41 and 8.4 + 4.1 = 12.5% of these are caused by liver disease caused by alcohol use and intentional self-harm. 12.5% of 1,160 = 1,160 ÷ 100 = 11.60 × 12.5 = 145.

15. Answer B, Multiply 95,294 × 0.002629 and subtract the total from 95,294

Explanation: Suggested Answer D will calculate the number of deaths. To find the survivors you must subtract the deaths that year from the survivors as described in suggested Answer B.

Data set 4

16. Answer C, 8.625%

Explanation: The borrower rate in the example is given as 8.67% but this would be adjusted to the nearest 1/8 %; 5/8 = 0.625, 6/8 = 0.75 so the actual rate would be 8.625%.

17. Answer A, 37%

Explanation: 100% = 4.2 billion – 2.646 = 1.554 billion decrease, 1.554 ÷ 4.2 = 0.37 × 100 = 37%.

18. Answer D, $260 million

Explanation: Each week there are 20,000 new accounts and the average deposit is $13,000. Find the weekly total deposits by multiplying 20,000 × 13,000 = 260 million.

19. Answer B, 3.875%

Explanation: New depositor rate 1.92 + margin 2.00 = 3.92 borrow rate rounded to the nearest 1/8% = (7/8 = 0.875) = 3.875%.

20. Answer C, $50

Explanation: The Bank of Granite borrower rate 2008 was established in a previous question = 8.625%. The new borrower rate = 8.125% = 0.5% difference, 10,000 × 0.005 = $50.

Data set 5

21. Answer A, 74 cents

Explanation: We are told that the price of pasta doubled, $37 \times 2 = 74$ or 74 cents.

22. Answer D, 225%

Explanation: In the winter of 2006 the unit wholesale price was $40. This rose to $90 in the winter of 2007. 100% = 40, $90 \div 40$ = 2.25 × 100 = 225%.

23. Answer B, $1.11

Explanation: The new price $1.85 = old price × 1 and 2/3, so old price = 1.85 ÷ (1 and 2/3) approx 1.66.6% = approx 111.4; look to suggested answers to select B.

24. Answer A, 48.14%

Explanation: Apologies if you found this a misleading question and selected 'Cannot tell' because of the 'greater than' signs on two of the list. The information provided in the passage makes clear that all fruit and vegetables rose 1/3 and dairy products rose 2/3 so it is possible to answer the question. 1/3 is >0.33.3 and 2/3 is >66.6. So add the five values = 240.7 ÷ 5 to get 48.14%, the best estimate of the mean percentage increase.

25. Answer C, $1,500

Explanation: We are told that for every 9% increase in wholesale prices domestic bills increase 1%. We have established that wholesale prices increased by 225% ÷ 9 = 25% so the $300 increase = 25% increase on the previous bill. If 300 = 25% then 1% (300 ÷ 25) = 12 and 100% = 1200 + the 300 increase, meaning that the average annual gas bill rose to $1,500.

Data set 6

26. Answer A, 12 lb

Explanation: Overweight starts at a BMI of 25, 6′ = 72″ = overweight at 171 lb, 5′9″ = 69″ = overweight at 159 lb = 12 lb difference.

27. Answer B, 5′4″

Explanation: Average woman = 162.56 cm and 1 inch = 2.54 cm; find the inches: 162.56 ÷ 2.54 = 64″ or 5′4″ (speed up this calculation by dividing by 2.50 and selecting the nearest (lower) suggested answer).

28. Answer D, 1,300

Explanation: Find 32.5% of 4,000, 4,000 = 100%, 1% = 40, 32.5 × 40 = 32.5% of 4,000 = 1,300.

29. Answer C, 16 lb

Explanation: Obese = BMI of 30 or greater, woman 5′6″ = 66″ is obese at 172 lb or more, the woman weighs 187 lb so must lose more than 15 lb to avoid classification of obese, therefore Answer C, 16 lb.

30. Answer A, 23

Explanation: A man of average height = 175.26cm ÷ 2.54 = 69″; 67.6kg × 2.204 = (rounded to the nearest whole) 149 lb, a man 69″ tall weighing 149 lb would have a BMI of 23.